Harvesting Illusions:
The Global Greed and the Pan-African Paradox

A Manifesto Against Greed

Harvesting Illusions: The Global Greed and the Pan-African Paradox

Kayumba David

Published by Kayumba David, 2024.

While every precaution has been taken in the preparation of this book, the publisher assumes no responsibility for errors or omissions, or for damages resulting from the use of the information contained herein.

HARVESTING ILLUSIONS: THE GLOBAL GREED AND THE PAN-AFRICAN PARADOX

First edition. November 9, 2024.

ISBN: 979-8227937452

Written by Kayumba David.

Also by Kayumba David

1
Grow a Backbone and Walk out of an Abusive Marriage

Standalone
Cry Africa The Western Guide on How Not to Fail the Continent
Grow a Backbone and Walk out of an Abusive Marriage
Hope and Healing: A Chaplain's Handbook
Visas: The Irony of Freedom
A Meeting with Majesty: The King's Call to Humanity
Visas: The Irony of Freedom
Love Beyond Time A Comedy of Divine Connection
Silent Complicity: State Sovereignty, Global Inaction, and the
Rwandan Genocide
Bridging the Rift: A Pacifist Vision for the Israel-Palestine Future
Thanks to Calvary: A Salvific Treatise on the Cross
The centuries old swindlers
Harvesting Illusions: The Global Greed and the Pan-African Paradox
Hope and Recovery - A Chaplain's Handbook
The Only Crying God in all the Universe
LGBTQ Debunked by Natural Law
The Scandal of Gentleness: Who Was Jesus?

Kayumba David Kay

The Earth Is Not Harvestable, We Only Harvest Its Leaves

2

Copyright

© 2024 bykayumba David

Published by Kay Publications

Preface

In a world where the relentless pursuit of wealth and power has overshadowed the fundamental values of compassion, sustainability, and equity, this book serves as a satirical mirror reflecting our collective absurdities.

Through the lens of sarcasm and irony, we delve into the grand illusion of ownership, the deceptive allure of progress, and the hollow promises of those who hold the reins of power. It is a call to reevaluate our priorities, to shift our focus from exploitation to stewardship, and to embrace a future where the true measure of success is not how much we take, but how much we give back.

This book is dedicated to the less privileged of this world who struggle to live, to those whose daily lives are marked by resilience in the face of systemic inequities. May their struggles inspire us to create a world where justice, equity, and sustainability are not mere ideals, but lived realities.

Introduction

Harvesting Illusions: The Global Greed and the Pan-African Paradox

Welcome to a book that doesn't just skim the surface of the world's absurdities but plunges headfirst into the deep end, all while wearing a smile of biting sarcasm. This is a manifesto for anyone who's ever looked at the state of our planet, our leaders, and our so-called progress, and wondered, "Is this really the best we can do?"

In this book, we'll explore two interwoven themes that, at first glance, may seem worlds apart, but are, in reality, two sides of the same tarnished coin. First, we'll dive into the global obsession with greed—the relentless, unquenchable thirst to harvest the Earth as if it were an all-you-can-eat buffet, while ignoring the simple truth that the planet isn't something we can own or exhaust. It's a borrowed treasure, one that we're rapidly squandering in our race to accumulate wealth that, in the end, is as transient as a summer breeze. This section lays bare the absurdity of the human condition, where politicians, corporations, and even ordinary citizens partake in a collective delusion of ownership, all while forgetting that life's greatest riches can't be measured in dollars, pounds, or euros.

But the critique doesn't stop there. In the second section, we turn our gaze to Africa, where the paradox of progress is perhaps most starkly evident. This section is an exploration of **The Pan-African Paradox**—a deep dive into the curious case of leaders like Uganda's long-serving president, Yoweri Museveni. Museveni's story, emblematic of so many on the continent, is one of a revolutionary turned autocrat, a liberator turned oppressor. He symbolizes the betrayal of post-colonial Africa's promise, where dreams of unity and development have too often given way to tyranny, corruption, and a staggering gap between the powerful and the powerless.

We examine how, in Uganda and beyond, the promise of independence and progress has been co-opted by leaders who, having fought for freedom, now cling to power with all the tenacity of those they once opposed. They have mastered the art of manipulating systems, buying loyalty, and amassing wealth, all while their nations remain mired in poverty and underdevelopment. And yet, these leaders, for all their power and wealth, are as bound by the same laws of nature as the rest of us. Life is fleeting, death inevitable, and no amount of influence or gold can alter that fundamental truth.

But what if, instead of continuing down this path of greed and exploitation, we chose a different way? What if we stopped trying to harvest the Earth and its people for all they're worth and started focusing on what truly matters: building communities, nurturing the planet, and ensuring that everyone has enough—not just the privileged few? This book asks the uncomfortable questions, challenging the reader to look beyond the surface and see the futility of our current trajectory.

We'll reflect on the words of the master teacher, Jesus, who wisely asked, "What shall it profit a man to gain the whole world but lose his soul?" And we'll embrace the Ubuntu philosophy, which reminds us that "I am because you are, and we are because you are." These timeless truths offer a stark contrast to the hollow pursuits of wealth and power that dominate our world today.

In the end, this book is a call to wake up from the collective delusion we've been sold—a call to recognize that the Earth is not harvestable; we only harvest its leaves. And that's enough. It's a manifesto against greed, a plea for sanity in an insane world, and a reminder that the most valuable things in life are not things at all, but the connections we share and the legacy we leave behind.

So, buckle up, dear reader. This is not just a book; it's a journey through the absurd, the tragic, and the painfully real. It's a sarcastic manifesto that seeks to peel back the layers of illusion that define our modern world and expose the truth beneath. And perhaps, if we're lucky, it will inspire a few of us to start planting seeds of change in the fertile ground of what really matters.

Note on the Structure of This Book

This book is thoughtfully divided into two distinct yet interconnected sections, each exploring the deeper truths about our world, our leadership, and our collective illusions.

Part I: Harvesting Illusions: The Global Greed and the Pan-African Paradox

This section delves into the global narrative of greed and the futility of our relentless pursuit to dominate the Earth. Through sharp wit and biting sarcasm, it examines the absurdity of trying to own and exploit a planet that we are merely borrowing. It challenges the myths of progress and wealth, revealing the transient nature of our pursuits and the hollow victories that come from prioritizing profit over people and the planet.

Part II: The Pan-African Paradox and the Illusion of Progress

In this section, we shift focus to Africa, where the promises of independence and unity have often been betrayed by those in power. Through the lens of the Pan-African experience, particularly the case of Uganda's President Yoweri Museveni, this section explores the contradictions of leadership and the persistent struggles for genuine progress on the continent. It highlights the paradox of leaders who once championed freedom but now perpetuate the same systems of oppression they once fought against.

Together, these sections offer a comprehensive critique of the world we live in, urging us to reconsider our values, our leaders, and the very notion of progress.

PART I OF THE BOOK

PROLOGUE

Welcome to the Harvest Festival

Welcome, dear reader, to the ultimate guide on how to suck the life out of our planet while pretending to care. Yes, you've stumbled upon a treasure trove of wisdom, a veritable cornucopia of strategies on how to exploit, deplete, and destroy everything in sight, all while maintaining a pristine public image. It's a masterclass in hypocrisy, brought to you by the very people who have turned greed into an art form.

Let's begin with the basics. We live in a world where "progress" is the magic word. It's the golden ticket that justifies every deforestation, every oil spill, and every displaced community. Who cares about the long-term consequences when there's money to be made and power to be amassed? The Earth is our playground, after all. If we're not stripping it of resources at breakneck speed, are we even doing it right?

Our esteemed leaders, the politicians, have shown us the way. These paragons of virtue have mastered the art of taking what doesn't belong to them and convincing the rest of us it's for our own good. They're like magicians, really. Watch as they pull wealth from thin air, not for the public, mind you, but for their own bottomless pockets. Bravo! It's a wonder they can sleep at night, but I suppose it helps when you have a mattress stuffed with cash.

And who could forget our corporate overlords? These titans of industry have figured out the secret to eternal wealth: exploit, deplete, repeat. They've turned the planet into a playground, and not the fun kind with swings and slides. No, this playground is one where only the richest kids get to play, while the rest of us watch from the sidelines, wondering if we'll ever get a turn. Spoiler alert: we won't.

But wait, there's more! While we're busy patting ourselves on the back for promoting climate change initiatives, let's ignore the inconvenient truth that millions of people are still going hungry. Why should we bother eliminating hunger when there's a whole planet out there to exploit? It's a futile struggle, after all. We can't possibly tackle more than one global crisis at a time. Let's just keep pretending that the Earth's finite resources can support our infinite greed.

In this book, we'll explore the grand illusion of ownership, the politician's paradise, the corporate conquest, the myth of progress, the fragility of life, the hollow mantra that sharing is caring, and finally, the real harvest. Spoiler: it's not what you think.

So here's to the dreamers, the idealists, the ones who believe that the Earth is more than just a resource to be exploited. Here's to the crazy notion that we can live in harmony with the planet, and with each other. It's a wild idea, I know. But if enough of us believe in it, maybe, just maybe, we can make it a reality. Because in the end, the Earth is not harvestable; we only harvest its leaves. And that's enough.

Now, grab your popcorn, sit back, and enjoy this delightful journey through the absurdities of our modern world. After all, if we can't laugh at our own self-destruction, what's left?

CHAPTER 1

The Grand Illusion of Ownership

Welcome to the age of enlightenment, where we've all been sold the dream of ownership. We've been convinced that we can own pieces of the Earth, as if it's a board game and we're all trying to buy Boardwalk. But here's the kicker: we don't own the Earth. At best, we're borrowing it, and even that's a generous way to put it. We're more like those pesky guests who overstay their welcome, leaving crumbs and chaos in our wake.

In this grand illusion of ownership, we've developed a collective amnesia about the natural world's true value. The forests, mountains, and rivers have existed long before us and will continue to do so long after we're gone. Yet, we've arrogantly claimed dominion over them, slapping our names on deeds and titles as if the Earth needs our permission to exist. It's a fantastical delusion, one that we've embraced with disturbing enthusiasm.

Our ancestors once understood the concept of stewardship. They knew they were part of a larger ecosystem, a web of life that required balance and respect. But somewhere along the way, we traded this wisdom for the shiny trinkets of progress and development. We replaced reverence with exploitation, turning sacred land into mere commodities.

Let's take a moment to reflect on the absurdity of it all. We spend our lives accumulating property, amassing land, and building empires, only to realize that we're mere blips on the geological timeline. The mountains we mine for precious metals, the forests we clear for agriculture, and the rivers we dam for power—they will outlast us by millennia. Our claims of ownership are laughable in the face of such timelessness.

Consider the sheer arrogance it takes to believe that a piece of paper can grant us control over nature. A land deed is just that—a piece of paper. It holds no power over the land itself. The Earth does not bow to our legal systems; it operates on a different plane of existence entirely. Our attempts to harness and control it are futile at best, destructive at worst.

This illusion of ownership also extends to the way we treat each other. Those with wealth and power accumulate vast amounts of land and resources, often at the expense of those with less. It's a game of Monopoly on a global scale, with the rich getting richer and the poor getting poorer. The idea that we can own and control the Earth fuels this cycle of inequality and exploitation.

We've built entire economies on the premise of ownership, creating wealth by extracting and depleting natural resources. We measure success by how much land we possess, how many properties we own, and how much we can accumulate. But this model is fundamentally flawed. It's based on the erroneous belief that the Earth's resources are infinite, that there will always be more to take. In reality, we're depleting our planet at an alarming rate, jeopardizing the future of generations to come.

The consequences of this mindset are all around us. Climate change, deforestation, soil erosion, and biodiversity loss are just a few of the signs that we've pushed our planet to its limits. We're on a collision course with disaster, all because we refuse to acknowledge the limits of our so-called ownership. The Earth is not a bottomless well we can draw from indefinitely. It's a living, breathing entity that needs our respect and care.

But what if we shifted our perspective? What if we saw ourselves not as owners, but as caretakers? This shift would require a fundamental change in how we view our relationship with the Earth and each other. It would mean recognizing that we are part of a larger whole, that our well-being is intertwined with the health of our planet.

It would mean valuing sustainability over exploitation, cooperation over competition.

Imagine a world where we live in harmony with nature, where we take only what we need and give back more than we take. A world where we prioritize the health of our ecosystems and the well-being of all living creatures. This is not a utopian dream; it's a necessity if we are to survive and thrive as a species.

The first step towards this new paradigm is acknowledging the grand illusion of ownership for what it is—a myth. We do not own the Earth; we are merely its temporary custodians. Our time here is fleeting, but our impact can be lasting. Let's make it a positive one. Let's move from a mindset of ownership to one of stewardship, from exploitation to restoration. Only then can we hope to leave a legacy worth inheriting.

CHAPTER 2

The Politician's Paradise

Let's give a round of applause to our dear politicians, shall we? These are the folks who've mastered the art of taking what doesn't belong to them and convincing the rest of us it's for our own good. They're like magicians, really. Watch as they pull wealth from thin air, not for the public, mind you, but for their own bottomless pockets. Bravo! It's a wonder they can sleep at night, but I suppose it helps when you have a mattress stuffed with cash.

Ah, politicians, the maestros of manipulation, the virtuosos of verbosity. They have an uncanny ability to transform personal ambition into public service, at least in their carefully crafted speeches. With a flick of their silver tongues, they can turn policies designed to line their own pockets into grand crusades for the common good. It's a performance worthy of the finest stage, complete with theatrics, deception, and a captivated audience.

These public servants, as they like to call themselves, have perfected the art of double-speak. When they say "public interest," what they really mean is "my interest." When they promise transparency, it's usually behind the most opaque curtains of bureaucracy. And when they talk about serving the people, they often mean serving themselves an extra helping of the pie. It's a masterclass in saying one thing and doing another, a talent honed over years of practice and deceit.

Take, for instance, the grand promises they make during election campaigns. Jobs for everyone, healthcare for all, a cleaner environment, safer streets, and so on. These promises are like balloons, bright and full of hot air. But as soon as the election is over, they pop, leaving nothing but the sound of our collective disappointment echoing in the air. It's a classic bait-and-switch, and we fall for it every single time.

Let's not forget their favorite trick: the diversion. Whenever there's a scandal or a failure that's too glaring to ignore, they simply shift our attention to something else. A new enemy, a fresh crisis, a different scandal—anything to keep us from focusing on their shortcomings. It's like watching a shell game, where the goal is to keep our eyes moving so fast we forget to question why the ball isn't under any of the cups.

These political wizards also have a remarkable knack for self-preservation. No matter how dire the situation, they always manage to come out unscathed. Financial crisis? They've got golden parachutes. Environmental disaster? They're safely ensconced in their climate-controlled mansions. War? Their children are far from the front lines. They navigate the storms they help create with the ease of seasoned sailors, leaving the rest of us to sink or swim.

The irony is that while they enrich themselves, they perpetuate the myth that they are sacrificing for the greater good. They attend ribbon-cutting ceremonies, make grand speeches, and shake hands with the very people they're exploiting. They wear the mantle of leadership like a costume, donning it when it's convenient and discarding it when it's not. It's a performance, plain and simple, and we're the unwitting audience.

And let's talk about their insatiable appetite for power and wealth. These politicians often enter office with modest means and leave as multi-millionaires. Their secret? Insider knowledge, shady deals, and the revolving door between government and industry. They write laws that benefit their future employers, knowing full well they'll be handsomely rewarded once they leave office. It's a rigged system, designed to benefit those who know how to play the game.

But perhaps the most egregious act is their ability to sleep at night. One might wonder how they manage to find rest while the world around them burns, but then again, it's easy to sleep when you're cushioned by the spoils of your deceit. They lie down on mattresses stuffed with cash, close their eyes to the suffering outside their gilded walls, and dream of the next big score. Their conscience is as empty as their promises.

In this politician's paradise, the needs of the many are always secondary to the desires of the few. The public trust is a currency to be traded, the environment a resource to be exploited, and the future a problem for someone else to solve. They've mastered the art of plausible deniability, always having an excuse, a scapegoat, or a deflection at the ready. It's a well-oiled machine, and it grinds on relentlessly.

But what if we, the people, decided to stop being the audience to this tragic play? What if we demanded accountability, transparency, and genuine public service? It would mean dismantling the illusion, pulling back the curtain, and exposing the charlatans for who they really are. It would mean holding them to their promises and making sure that they serve us, not themselves.

In the end, the politician's paradise is a mirage, a fleeting illusion sustained by our complacency. It's time to wake up, see through the smoke and mirrors, and reclaim our power. Because the true paradise is not one built on lies and greed, but on honesty, integrity, and genuine care for the common good. Let's stop applauding their deceit and start demanding the truth. Only then can we hope to create a world where public service truly serves the public.

CHAPTER 3

The Corporate Conquest

And who could forget our friends in the corporate world? These titans of industry have figured out the secret to eternal wealth: exploit, deplete, repeat. They've turned the planet into a playground, and not the fun kind with swings and slides. No, this playground is one where only the richest kids get to play, while the rest of us watch from the sidelines, wondering if we'll ever get a turn. Spoiler alert: we won't.

Let's take a moment to admire the sheer audacity of these corporate juggernauts. They've managed to convince us that their relentless pursuit of profit is somehow in our best interest. They've turned exploitation into an art form, masking their greed with slick marketing campaigns and corporate social responsibility reports. They sponsor a few charity events, plant a couple of trees, and suddenly they're the heroes of the modern age. Never mind the environmental devastation, the human rights abuses, or the economic inequalities they perpetuate. Those are just minor inconveniences in the grand scheme of things.

These corporations operate like well-oiled machines, optimizing every aspect of their operations for maximum profit. Efficiency, they call it. But what they really mean is squeezing every last drop of value from their workers, their resources, and their markets. They treat their employees like expendable cogs in a giant money-making machine, paying them just enough to keep them coming back but never enough to truly prosper. The promise of advancement and success dangles just out of reach, keeping the workforce motivated and compliant.

And let's not overlook their environmental footprint. The corporate world has perfected the art of externalizing costs. Pollution? Someone else's problem. Resource depletion? Future generations will deal with it. Habitat destruction? Just a necessary sacrifice for progress. They bulldoze forests, pollute rivers, and pump greenhouse gases into the atmosphere, all in the name of growth and shareholder value. The Earth is nothing more than a resource to be exploited, a giant piggy bank to be cracked open and emptied.

The corporate conquest extends beyond the environment and into our very lives. They've commodified our time, our attention, and even our relationships. Social media giants harvest our data, turning our personal lives into profit streams. Retail behemoths exploit consumer psychology, manipulating us into buying things we don't need with money we don't have. The gig economy giants have convinced us that precarious, underpaid work is the new normal. We're not citizens anymore; we're consumers, and our value is measured by how much we spend.

These corporate titans also have a stranglehold on our political systems. Through lobbying, campaign donations, and the revolving door between government and industry, they ensure that the rules of the game are always in their favor. Regulations that protect workers, consumers, and the environment are portrayed as job killers and innovation stiflers. Free markets, they argue, must remain unfettered to unleash their full potential. But what they really mean is that they must remain free to exploit, deplete, and repeat without interference.

The disparity between the corporate elite and the rest of us has never been greater. The CEOs and shareholders reap the rewards of our collective labor, living in opulence while the rest of us struggle to make ends meet. The wealth gap widens, and the American Dream slips further out of reach for the majority. We're told that if we just work hard enough, we too can join the ranks of the elite. But the game is rigged, and the odds are stacked against us.

This exploitation extends to the global south, where the quest for resources like diamonds and coltan turns deadly. The phrase "blood diamonds" isn't just a metaphor—it's a stark reality. Diamonds mined in conflict zones, particularly in Africa, fund brutal wars and human rights abuses. Armed groups force locals into labor, using violence and terror to maintain control. The precious stones are then sold on the international market, where their bloody origins are often obscured by layers of transactions.

Coltan, a mineral essential for modern electronics, tells a similar story. In countries like the Democratic Republic of Congo, coltan mining fuels conflict and exploitation. Militias battle for control of mining areas, subjecting workers, often children, to dangerous conditions for meager wages. The wealth generated from coltan flows not to the impoverished communities but to warlords and their Western corporate backers. This vicious cycle of exploitation and violence is a hidden cost of our technological advancements.

These resource-driven conflicts are exacerbated by African dictators who, in collusion with multinational corporations, siphon off the wealth for themselves. Western corporations, hungry for resources, turn a blind eye to the atrocities, their only concern being the steady flow of raw materials. In return, they support these dictators, providing the financial backing and legitimacy needed to maintain their regimes. The local population, meanwhile, remains trapped in poverty and violence, their land and labor stolen for the benefit of the few.

So, what can we do in the face of such overwhelming power? First, we must recognize the illusion for what it is. The corporate conquest is not an inevitable byproduct of progress; it's a deliberate choice made by those in power. We need to challenge the narrative that equates corporate success with societal success. True progress means ensuring that everyone, not just the privileged few, has access to the opportunities and resources they need to thrive.

We can start by demanding greater accountability and transparency from these corporations. They must be held responsible for their environmental and social impacts. We need stronger regulations, not weaker ones, to protect our planet and our communities. We can support businesses that prioritize sustainability and ethical practices, putting our money where our values are. And we must advocate for policies that promote economic equality, such as fair wages, progressive taxation, and robust social safety nets.

Ultimately, we need to redefine what success looks like. It's not about endless growth and accumulation; it's about well-being, sustainability, and equity. The corporate conquest has brought us to the brink, but it's not too late to change course. By standing together and demanding a fairer, more just system, we can reclaim our future from the clutches of corporate greed. The playground belongs to all of us, not just the richest kids on the block. It's time we all got a turn.

CHAPTER 4

The Myth of Progress

Progress. It's a word that gets thrown around a lot, usually by those who are making the most money from it. We're told that all this development, all this destruction, is necessary for the greater good. But whose good are we talking about? The good of the many, or the good of the few? If you guessed the latter, congratulations! You've been paying attention.

Let's explore this so-called progress through the lens of African history, where the tale of underdevelopment is particularly stark. For centuries, the continent has been the target of exploitation, first through the slave trade, then colonialism, and now the modern iterations of economic imperialism.

During the transatlantic slave trade, millions of Africans were forcibly taken from their homeland, their lives and communities shattered. This brutal period not only decimated populations but also disrupted the development of African societies. Entire regions were destabilized as the strongest members of communities were torn away, leaving behind a landscape of trauma and fragmentation.

The advent of colonialism only deepened the wounds. European powers carved up Africa with little regard for existing cultural and ethnic boundaries, creating artificial states that were easier to control. Under colonial rule, African resources were systematically extracted for the benefit of European industries. The Congo Free State under King Leopold II of Belgium is a grim example.

Millions of Congolese died from forced labor, disease, and starvation as Leopold's regime exploited the region's rubber and ivory resources. This is the legacy of progress according to the colonial playbook: wealth for the colonizers, death and devastation for the colonized.

Even after gaining independence, many African nations found themselves ensnared in a new form of economic colonialism. Structural adjustment programs imposed by the International Monetary Fund (IMF) and the World Bank in the 1980s and 1990s are prime examples.

These programs, touted as necessary for economic progress, forced African countries to cut public spending, privatize state-owned enterprises, and open up markets to foreign competition. The result? Deteriorating public services, increased poverty, and heightened inequality. The myth of progress, once again, served the interests of a wealthy few at the expense of the many.

Consider the case of Ghana. In the early 1980s, under pressure from the IMF, Ghana adopted structural adjustment policies. Public sector workers were laid off, health and education budgets were slashed, and subsidies for farmers were removed. While these measures were intended to stabilize the economy and spur growth, the immediate impact was severe hardship for the majority of Ghanaians. Health indicators declined, literacy rates stagnated, and income inequality soared. The so-called progress came at an unbearable human cost.

In more recent years, the exploitation has continued under the guise of globalization. Multinational corporations extract valuable minerals and resources from African soil, often with the complicity of local elites. Take the example of the Niger Delta in Nigeria, where oil extraction by foreign companies has led to environmental catastrophe and human suffering. Oil spills have devastated fishing communities, polluted water sources, and caused widespread health problems. Yet, the profits from this industry rarely benefit the local population. Instead, they flow out of Nigeria, enriching foreign shareholders and a small cohort of local elites.

The painful survival of the black race in the face of these ongoing assaults is a testament to resilience. Despite the relentless exploitation and systemic underdevelopment, African people continue to find ways to thrive. They build communities, preserve cultures, and innovate in the face of adversity. However, this resilience is often overlooked in the dominant narrative of progress, which prefers to focus on GDP growth and foreign investment rather than human well-being and social equity.

The myth of progress also manifests in the portrayal of technology and modernization as universally beneficial. But technology can be a double-edged sword. For instance, while mobile banking has transformed financial access in many parts of Africa, it has also facilitated predatory lending practices. Digital loan platforms, often backed by Western investors, charge exorbitant interest rates, trapping low-income users in cycles of debt. The technological progress celebrated in boardrooms and tech conferences often translates to new forms of exploitation on the ground.

So, whose progress are we really talking about? For every skyscraper built, how many communities are displaced? For every percentage point increase in GDP, how many more people fall below the poverty line? The benefits of this so-called progress are not evenly distributed. They accrue to the powerful and the wealthy, while the majority are left to deal with the fallout.

The painful reality of African underdevelopment and the survival of its people amidst ongoing exploitation highlights the need to redefine progress. True progress should be measured by the well-being of all people, the health of our environment, and the fairness of our social systems. It should uplift the many, not just the privileged few. Until we achieve this, progress remains a myth—a story told by the powerful to justify their wealth and control.

It's time to shatter this myth and create a new narrative. One where progress is inclusive, equitable, and sustainable. One where the development of African nations is driven by the needs and aspirations of their people, not the profit motives of foreign corporations and local elites. Only then can we speak of genuine progress, one that benefits everyone, not just the fortunate few.

to the above add the following: Why should the leaders crave for more wealth at the expense of the poor masses. Does greed really brings lasting peace?

CHAPTER 5

The Fragility of Life

Life is short. A cliché, but like most clichés, it's true. We're here for a moment, and then we're gone. Yet, in that brief time, some people manage to accumulate wealth and power as if they're planning to take it with them. Newsflash: there are no pockets in shrouds. All that greed, all that hoarding, it amounts to nothing in the end. So why do it? Maybe because it's the only game they know how to play.

Consider the case of Genghis Khan, the fearsome Mongol leader who carved out the largest contiguous empire in history. Genghis Khan amassed vast territories and untold wealth through brutal conquests and unrelenting warfare. At the height of his power, he controlled much of Asia and Europe, ruling over millions. Yet, despite all his power and riches, Genghis Khan could not escape the inevitability of death. When he died in 1227, his vast empire quickly fragmented, and his wealth scattered. His ambition and greed left a legacy of destruction and division rather than lasting peace and prosperity.

Fast forward to the 20th century, and we encounter John D. Rockefeller, the American oil magnate. Rockefeller became one of the wealthiest individuals in history by monopolizing the oil industry through his company, Standard Oil. His fortune was so immense that it accounted for over 1% of the U.S. economy at its peak. Yet, despite his immense wealth, Rockefeller faced health issues and spent the latter part of his life giving away much of his fortune to philanthropy. His attempts to control and harvest the Earth's resources ultimately brought him little personal happiness or peace. He is remembered as much for his ruthless business practices as for his charitable contributions.

Another example is Ferdinand Marcos, the former dictator of the Philippines. Marcos ruled the country with an iron fist from 1965 to

1986, amassing vast wealth through corruption, embezzlement, and the exploitation of his people. His regime was marked by widespread human rights abuses and economic mismanagement. Despite his immense wealth and power, Marcos was eventually overthrown and died in exile. His ill-gotten gains could not shield him from the consequences of his actions, and his legacy is one of infamy and disgrace.

More recently, we have seen the case of Muammar Gaddafi, the Libyan leader who ruled for over four decades. Gaddafi amassed a fortune estimated in the billions, much of it siphoned from Libya's oil wealth. His lavish lifestyle and brutal repression of dissent made him one of the world's most infamous dictators. In the end, Gaddafi was overthrown and killed during the Libyan Civil War in 2011. His wealth and power could not save him from a violent and ignominious death, nor could they prevent the subsequent chaos and suffering in Libya.

These powerful individuals, despite their immense wealth and influence, could not escape the fragility of life. Their attempts to harvest the Earth's resources and accumulate power ultimately amounted to nothing in the face of mortality. Their legacies are often tainted by the suffering they caused and the fleeting nature of their achievements.

The fragility of life is a reminder that our true impact lies not in how much we accumulate but in how we contribute to the world around us. Consider the contrasting example of Nelson Mandela. Mandela, who spent 27 years in prison for his fight against apartheid, emerged not with a fortune, but with a vision of reconciliation and justice. His legacy is not one of wealth, but of profound social change and the enduring hope he inspired in millions.

Another stark contrast is Mother Teresa, who dedicated her life to serving the poorest of the poor in India. She had no material wealth, yet her impact on the world was immense. Her life's work demonstrated that true richness comes from compassion and service to others, not from the accumulation of wealth and power.

Why then do so many powerful individuals fall into the trap of greed and accumulation? Perhaps it's because the pursuit of wealth and power is a tangible goal in a world that often feels uncertain and fleeting. It provides a sense of control and significance, however temporary. But as the stories of Genghis Khan, Rockefeller, Marcos, and Gaddafi show, this pursuit is ultimately hollow. The peace and security they sought through wealth and power proved illusory.

The fragility of life urges us to reconsider our priorities. Instead of hoarding wealth and resources, we should focus on building communities, fostering relationships, and contributing to the well-being of others. True peace and fulfillment come not from what we take from the Earth, but from what we give back. The Earth is not a treasure chest to be emptied; it is a home to be nurtured and shared.

In the end, the measure of our lives is not the wealth we accumulate but the legacy we leave behind. The powerful individuals who tried to harvest the Earth in vain serve as cautionary tales. Their lives remind us that our time here is limited and that our true impact lies in how we treat others and the planet we share. It's a lesson we would do well to heed, for the sake of our own fulfillment and the future of generations to come.

CHAPTER 6

Sharing is Caring (But Not Really)

We teach children that sharing is caring, and then we grow up and forget all about it. Or maybe we remember but choose to ignore it. After all, sharing means having less, and having less means not winning. And isn't life all about winning? About having more than the next person, about being the king of the hill? But here's the secret: the hill is an illusion, and there's no prize at the top.

From a young age, we instill in our children the value of sharing. We encourage them to share their toys, their snacks, and their time with others. We tell them that sharing is a fundamental part of being a good person. But as they grow older, the message becomes muddled. The world they encounter values competition and accumulation far more than cooperation and generosity. The once clear concept that sharing is essential to community and kindness gets overshadowed by the relentless pursuit of personal success.

In the adult world, sharing is often seen as a sign of weakness or naivety. The corporate culture celebrates those who climb the ladder the fastest, even if it means stepping on others along the way. The business mogul who amasses billions is lauded, while the philanthropist who gives away millions is often viewed with skepticism. We're told that to succeed, we must look out for number one, because nobody else will.

Consider the disparity in wealth distribution globally. According to Oxfam, the world's richest 1% have more than twice as much wealth as 6.9 billion people. This staggering inequality is a direct result of a system that rewards hoarding and penalizes sharing. The rich get richer, not because they work harder, but because they play by different rules—rules designed to maintain their wealth and power.

Let's look at the tech industry, where billionaires like Jeff Bezos and Elon Musk epitomize this culture of accumulation. Bezos, the founder of Amazon, has built an empire that spans the globe. Yet, despite his vast wealth, Amazon is notorious for its poor working conditions and minimal wages for warehouse employees. Sharing the wealth with those who actually help generate it would seem logical, but it contradicts the ethos of maximizing personal gain. Musk, on the other hand, while championing innovation and sustainability, often skirts the issue of fair labor practices and equitable profit distribution. Both men are on top of their respective hills, but the cost of their ascent is borne by those at the bottom.

On a societal level, the concept of sharing extends to public services and welfare. Scandinavian countries, known for their high quality of life, operate on principles of extensive social sharing. High taxes fund universal healthcare, education, and robust social safety nets. These countries understand that societal well-being improves when resources are shared equitably. Contrast this with countries like the United States, where the mere mention of universal healthcare sparks fierce debate. The idea of sharing wealth through taxation to provide basic services for all is met with cries of socialism and threats to personal freedom.

The irony is that, despite the relentless pursuit of individual wealth, true fulfillment often comes from giving rather than receiving. Studies consistently show that acts of generosity and sharing boost our well-being. The joy of helping others, of contributing to something larger than ourselves, provides a deeper sense of satisfaction than any amount of money or material possessions. Yet, this wisdom is often drowned out by the cultural narrative that equates success with accumulation.

The concept of the hill, this supposed pinnacle of success, is a powerful metaphor. We strive to reach the top, believing it holds the ultimate reward. We compete fiercely, often ruthlessly, to outdo our peers. But when we finally reach the summit, we find it empty. There is no prize, no lasting fulfillment, just a lonely peak surrounded by those we've alienated in our climb. The hill is an illusion, a false promise that leads us away from the true sources of happiness and contentment.

What if we redefined success? What if, instead of valuing those who accumulate the most, we celebrated those who share the most? What if our heroes were not the billionaires, but the teachers, the social workers, the community leaders who dedicate their lives to improving the lives of others? This shift in values could transform our society, fostering a culture where sharing is genuinely seen as caring, not just a platitude for children.

This isn't to say that ambition and personal success are inherently wrong. Aspiring to improve oneself and achieve personal goals is a natural and healthy part of life. However, when personal success comes at the expense of others, when it fosters inequality and perpetuates suffering, it becomes toxic. True progress involves lifting others as we climb, ensuring that our success contributes to the collective good rather than detracting from it.

In a world where sharing is genuinely valued, resources would be more equitably distributed, and opportunities would be available to all, not just the privileged few. We would recognize that our well-being is interconnected and that helping others ultimately helps us all. The wealthiest among us would understand that their fortunes are built on the contributions of many and would feel a responsibility to give back, to share their success in meaningful ways.

The lesson we teach children—that sharing is caring—is not just a moral nicety; it's a fundamental truth about how to create a just and sustainable world. It's a lesson we need to relearn as adults, to move beyond the illusion of the hill and seek a more inclusive, equitable form of success. Only then can we build a society where everyone has the opportunity to thrive, where the true meaning of sharing is understood and embraced by all.

CHAPTER 7

The Real Harvest

What if, instead of trying to harvest the Earth for everything it's got, we focused on something else? What if we tried to harvest happiness, community, sustainability? I know, it sounds crazy. But maybe, just maybe, it's worth a try. Because in the end, it's not about how much we can take, but how much we can give. Not about the wealth we accumulate, but the legacy we leave behind.

Imagine a world where our primary goal is not to extract as much as possible from the planet, but to cultivate well-being, foster connections, and ensure a sustainable future. This shift in perspective could transform our societies, economies, and our very way of life. It's a radical idea, but it's also a necessary one if we hope to create a world that is not only livable but thriving for future generations.

Let's start with the concept of harvesting happiness. In many cultures, happiness is mistakenly equated with material wealth and consumption. But true happiness often comes from intangible sources: meaningful relationships, a sense of purpose, and connection to our communities. Studies have shown that beyond a certain point, increases in income do not correlate with increases in happiness. In fact, the pursuit of wealth can lead to stress, anxiety, and a sense of emptiness.

Countries like Bhutan have recognized this and have implemented policies that prioritize Gross National Happiness over Gross Domestic Product. This approach considers factors such as psychological well-being, health, education, time use, cultural diversity, good governance, community vitality, ecological diversity, and living standards. By focusing on these areas, Bhutan seeks to create a society where happiness and well-being are at the forefront of national development.

Next, let's consider the idea of harvesting community. In many parts of the world, especially in urban environments, people feel increasingly isolated despite being surrounded by others. The breakdown of community structures has led to a rise in loneliness and a decrease in social cohesion. But what if we invested in rebuilding our communities? This could involve creating more public spaces where people can gather, fostering local organizations and events, and encouraging civic engagement.

Strong communities provide a support network that can help individuals through tough times and contribute to a sense of belonging and identity. They can also drive local initiatives that address specific needs and challenges, leading to more resilient and adaptable societies. When people feel connected and supported, they are more likely to contribute positively to their community, creating a virtuous cycle of mutual benefit.

Sustainability is another crucial area where we can shift our focus. The current model of endless consumption and growth is not only unsustainable but also destructive. We are depleting natural resources at an alarming rate, causing irreversible damage to ecosystems and contributing to climate change. But what if we prioritized sustainability in all aspects of our lives? This would involve rethinking how we produce and consume goods, transitioning to renewable energy sources, and adopting practices that protect and restore our environment.

Sustainability also means considering the long-term impacts of our actions. Instead of focusing on short-term gains, we need to think about the legacy we are leaving for future generations. This could involve investing in education and innovation to develop new technologies and solutions that reduce our environmental footprint. It could also mean supporting policies and initiatives that promote sustainable development and conservation efforts.

Yet, while the world tries to promote climate change mitigation strategies, a glaring issue often remains unaddressed: the elimination of hunger. How can we expect to create a sustainable future when millions of people around the world still struggle to meet their basic nutritional needs? The struggle to combat climate change can seem futile when basic human rights, such as access to food, are not met.

The paradox is evident. Climate change initiatives, like transitioning to renewable energy or adopting sustainable agriculture, are crucial. However, without addressing the immediate needs of the hungry, these efforts can appear misplaced. For instance, promoting plant-based diets or reducing meat consumption for environmental reasons may be a valid strategy in wealthier nations. Still, for communities where access to any food is a daily challenge, these discussions can seem out of touch with their realities.

To make real progress, we must recognize the interconnectedness of environmental sustainability and human well-being. We need holistic approaches that address both climate change and hunger simultaneously. This could mean implementing agricultural practices that not only reduce emissions but also increase food security. Agroecology, for example, emphasizes sustainable farming that improves soil health, increases biodiversity, and enhances food production, benefiting both the environment and local communities.

Take the example of initiatives in sub-Saharan Africa, where sustainable farming techniques have been introduced to improve food security and combat climate change. Projects that train farmers in agroforestry, crop diversification, and water conservation have shown promising results. These practices help restore degraded land, increase crop yields, and build resilience against climate impacts, all while ensuring that local communities have enough to eat.

Moreover, integrating food security into climate policies can create more robust and comprehensive strategies. For example, climate finance mechanisms can include provisions for supporting small-scale farmers and local food systems. By aligning climate goals with efforts to eliminate hunger, we can create synergies that address both crises more effectively.

The idea of harvesting happiness, community, and sustainability is not just about changing individual behaviors, but also about transforming our societal systems and values. It requires a collective effort to redefine what we consider valuable and to align our actions with these new priorities. This shift will not be easy, but it is essential if we hope to create a more just, equitable, and sustainable world.

Take, for example, the concept of the circular economy, which aims to design out waste and keep products and materials in use for as long as possible. This approach contrasts sharply with the traditional linear economy, where resources are extracted, used, and then discarded. By adopting circular principles, we can reduce our environmental impact, create new economic opportunities, and foster innovation.

Another example is the transition to renewable energy sources like solar, wind, and hydroelectric power. This shift not only helps to mitigate climate change but also creates jobs, reduces pollution, and enhances energy security. Countries that have embraced renewable energy, such as Denmark and Germany, have shown that it is possible to achieve economic growth while reducing carbon emissions and dependence on fossil fuels.

On a smaller scale, local initiatives can also have a significant impact. Community gardens, for instance, provide fresh produce, improve urban environments, and bring people together. They offer a space for residents to connect with nature, learn about sustainable practices, and build stronger community ties. Similarly, local currencies and time banking systems encourage local trade and support small businesses, fostering a more resilient and interconnected economy.

The real harvest lies in the intangible yet profoundly important aspects of life: the happiness we cultivate, the communities we build, and the sustainable practices we adopt. By shifting our focus from extraction and accumulation to giving and nurturing, we can create a legacy that enriches not just our lives, but the lives of others and the planet we all share.

In the end, the true measure of our success will not be the wealth we leave behind, but the positive impact we have had on the world. The real harvest is the lasting legacy of a life well-lived, one that prioritizes the well-being of people and the planet over the pursuit of endless growth and consumption. It's a vision worth striving for, and it starts with each of us, making choices that reflect our values and our hopes for the future.

EPILOGUE

A Call to Non-Action

So here's to the dreamers, the idealists, the ones who believe that the Earth is more than just a resource to be exploited. Here's to the crazy notion that we can live in harmony with the planet, and with each other. It's a wild idea, I know. But if enough of us believe in it, maybe, just maybe, we can make it a reality. Because in the end, the Earth is not harvestable; we only harvest its leaves. And that's enough.

In a world driven by relentless activity and constant consumption, the idea of non-action might seem counterintuitive, even radical. Yet, it is precisely this counter-cultural approach that offers a pathway to a more sustainable and equitable future. Non-action does not imply passivity or disengagement. Rather, it means reframing our relationship with the Earth and with each other, focusing on being rather than doing, and on nurturing rather than exploiting.

Consider the wisdom of indigenous cultures that have long understood the value of living in harmony with nature. These cultures view the Earth as a living entity to be respected and cared for, not as an inexhaustible resource to be plundered. They practice sustainable living, taking only what they need and ensuring that their actions support the health of their ecosystems. By embracing these principles of non-action, we can learn to tread more lightly on the Earth, honoring its limits and rhythms.

One profound example comes from the Awa people of the Amazon rainforest. They have lived sustainably in the rainforest for generations, their way of life intertwined with the natural world. They hunt and gather in ways that allow the forest to regenerate, ensuring that their needs do not deplete the resources they depend on. Their deep connection to the land demonstrates that it is possible to live richly and meaningfully without overwhelming exploitation.

In our modern context, adopting a philosophy of non-action means reevaluating what we truly need and prioritizing sustainability and well-being over consumption and growth. It means advocating for policies that protect natural resources, reduce waste, and promote renewable energy. It means supporting local economies and sustainable practices that nourish communities rather than deplete them. It means fostering a culture of care and stewardship, where the health of the planet and its inhabitants is valued above profit and production.

The call to non-action is also a call to mindfulness. It asks us to slow down, to be present, and to appreciate the simple, profound gifts that life offers. It encourages us to find joy in the small moments, in the beauty of a sunrise, the sound of birdsong, the feeling of the earth beneath our feet. By cultivating this awareness, we can develop a deeper appreciation for the natural world and a stronger commitment to protecting it.

Non-action challenges the dominant narrative that equates success with perpetual motion and accumulation. It invites us to redefine success in terms of balance, harmony, and sustainability. Imagine a world where progress is measured not by GDP, but by the health of our ecosystems, the happiness of our communities, and the resilience of our societies. This is the vision that non-action offers—a vision of a world where we live not in opposition to nature, but as part of it.

Achieving this vision requires collective effort and a fundamental shift in our values and behaviors. It means recognizing that we are all interconnected, that the well-being of one depends on the well-being of all. It means standing up to the forces of greed and exploitation, and advocating for a more just and equitable world. It means believing in the power of individuals and communities to make a difference, no matter how small their actions may seem.

The journey toward this new paradigm will not be easy. It will require courage, resilience, and a willingness to challenge the status quo. But it is a journey worth taking, for the sake of our planet and future generations. By embracing non-action, we can create a world where the Earth's resources are cherished and preserved, where communities thrive in harmony with their environment, and where the legacy we leave behind is one of care and stewardship.

So here's to the dreamers, the idealists, the visionaries. Here's to those who believe in the possibility of a better world, one where we live in balance with the Earth and with each other. Here's to the crazy notion that we can make this dream a reality, one step, one action, one moment of mindfulness at a time. Because in the end, the Earth is not harvestable; we only harvest its leaves. And that's enough.

As we move forward, let us carry this vision with us. Let us nurture it in our hearts and bring it to life through our actions. Let us remember that true wealth is not found in what we take from the Earth, but in what we give back. And let us commit to leaving a legacy of sustainability, equity, and peace. This is the real harvest—one that will nourish us all, now and in the generations to come.

PART II OF THE BOOK

Preface

The story of Uganda's President Yoweri Museveni is one of delightful contradictions. He speaks of unity with such passion that you might think he invented the concept, yet his policies often seem custom-designed to promote division. He champions Pan-Africanism with the fervor of a preacher at a revival meeting, but his treatment of certain groups within his own country tells a rather different tale. Ah, the sweet, sweet irony of it all.

Welcome to the theater of political paradox, starring none other than President Museveni, a man who has managed to become a symbol of Pan-African rhetoric while simultaneously undermining its core principles. It's a bit like watching a chef who insists on using the finest organic ingredients only to serve up fast food. The words are tantalizing, but the reality? Not so much.

Through a detailed examination of Museveni's tenure, particularly his relationship with the Banyarwanda people of Uganda, we will peel back the layers of political strategy and personal ambition that have defined his rule. Picture an onion, but instead of bringing tears to your eyes from chopping, this one will have you weeping from sheer exasperation.

This is not just a story about Uganda; it is a reflection of the broader challenges facing the Pan-African movement today. Museveni's antics offer a masterclass in how to wave the banner of unity while surreptitiously sowing discord. It is a call to examine the true meaning of unity and to challenge leaders who use it as a convenient cover for their own agendas.

So, dear reader, prepare yourself for a journey into the world of political theater, where grandiose speeches mask exclusionary practices and where the noble ideals of Pan-Africanism are twisted to serve personal ambition. It's a story that would be hilarious if it weren't so tragically true.

PROLOGUE

The Pan-African Paradox and the Illusion of Progress

Welcome to a book that dances between biting sarcasm and unsettling truths, a narrative that exposes the absurdity of our modern world while grappling with the deep contradictions that define it. This is a tale of two sections: one that critiques the destructive nature of greed and the fragility of life, and another that delves into the perplexing paradoxes of power and leadership, particularly within the Pan-African context. Together, these sections weave a story that is as frustrating as it is illuminating, as heartbreaking as it is darkly humorous.

In the first section, we embark on a journey through the landscapes of greed, exploitation, and the illusion of progress. We'll explore how the powerful have convinced themselves that they own the Earth, how politicians and corporations alike have mastered the art of taking what doesn't belong to them, and how the myth of progress has left entire continents, particularly Africa, in a perpetual state of underdevelopment. We'll reflect on the transient nature of wealth, the fragility of life, and the ultimate futility of trying to harvest the Earth's riches. With a tone dripping in sarcasm, we'll question the wisdom of those who hoard wealth and power, only to find that, in the end, they can't take any of it with them.

But this book doesn't stop at the global stage. In the second section, we turn our gaze to a more specific, yet equally perplexing phenomenon: **The Pan-African Paradox**. We'll delve into the curious case of Uganda's long-serving president, Yoweri Museveni, a leader who has come to symbolize the contradictions of African leadership.

Museveni, like many of his counterparts across the continent, once stood as a beacon of hope for a new, independent Africa. Yet, decades into his rule, Uganda faces many of the same challenges that have plagued it for generations: poverty, corruption, and a lack of true democratic governance.

Museveni's story is not unique. It is part of a broader narrative that has played out across the continent, where leaders who once fought for liberation and justice have become the very embodiment of the problems they sought to eradicate. These leaders have mastered the art of brandishing power as if they are immune to the inevitable march of time and death, clinging to their thrones while their nations suffer. They manipulate the machinery of the state to secure their positions, buying judges, falsifying information, and accumulating wealth, all the while ignoring the cries of their people.

And yet, amid all this, there remains a stubborn hope—hope that, despite the odds, something can change. This hope is not born from naivety but from the understanding that, as the master teacher Jesus once asked, "What shall it profit a man to gain the whole world but lose his soul?" In the Pan-African context, this question resonates deeply. It challenges leaders and citizens alike to reconsider what true progress means and to embrace the Ubuntu philosophy: "I am because you are, and we are because you are."

This book is dedicated to the less privileged of this world who struggle to live, who watch as the powerful play their games of wealth and dominance, and who, despite everything, continue to hope for a better tomorrow. It's a call to non-action for those who believe that maybe, just maybe, the best way to change the world is to stop trying to harvest it for all it's worth and start giving back, start building communities, and start seeing the Earth not as a resource to be exploited but as a home to be cherished.

So, as you turn the pages, let this book challenge your perceptions, provoke your thoughts, and perhaps even make you laugh at the absurdity of it all. But most importantly, let it remind you that in the end, the Earth is not harvestable; we only harvest its leaves. And that, my friends, is enough.

INTRODUCTION

Pan-Africanism has long been a symbol of unity and solidarity among African nations, a beacon of hope for a continent striving to break free from the shackles of colonialism and forge its own path. It is a vision of a united Africa, where borders are mere lines on a map and where the common heritage and shared struggles of its people bind them together. Yet, as with any grand vision, the reality on the ground often tells a different story.

Ah, Pan-Africanism. The glorious dream of a continent united, of people dancing hand-in-hand across national borders, celebrating their shared heritage, and forging a bright, collective future. What a lovely picture! But, alas, much like unicorns and pots of gold at the end of rainbows, this vision remains largely a figment of our imagination.

In the heart of East Africa lies Uganda, a nation with a complex history and a leader who has truly mastered the art of political maneuvering. President Yoweri Museveni, the self-proclaimed torchbearer of Pan-Africanism, stands at the center of this paradox. If you listen to his speeches, you might believe he single-handedly holds the keys to Africa's unity and prosperity. His rhetoric is filled with lofty ideals about solidarity, liberation, and brotherhood. It's enough to make one weep tears of joy and admiration – if only it weren't for that pesky thing called reality.

You see, Museveni's version of Pan-Africanism is a bit like a stage magician's act: all grand gestures and dramatic flair to distract from what's really happening behind the scenes. His speeches are masterpieces of highfalutin ideals, a veritable symphony of noble aspirations. And yet, when you peel back the layers of his rhetorical flourish, what do you find? A regime built on exclusion and division, cleverly masked by the language of unity.

This book delves into the curious case of Uganda's President, a man who has skillfully used the noble language of Pan-Africanism to mask a regime that thrives on xenophobia and marginalization. Welcome to the theatre of the absurd, where the protagonist, our esteemed President, plays the role of the Great Pan-African Pretender with unmatched finesse. Buckle up, dear reader, for this is a journey into the heart of a paradox where actions speak louder than words, and the truth is stranger – and far more disappointing – than the grandest fiction.

CHAPTER 1

The Great Pan-African Pretender

Ah, Uganda's esteemed President, the self-proclaimed beacon of Pan-African unity. If there were an award for the most flamboyant Pan-Africanist rhetoric, he would undoubtedly be the undisputed champion. His speeches are a masterclass in highfalutin ideals about the solidarity of the black man, the emancipation of Africa from neo-colonial chains, and the utopian vision of a united Africa. And yet, like a magician pulling a rabbit out of a hat, he manages to distract the audience from the rather inconvenient reality right under his nose.

Picture this: a grand stage adorned with the colors of the African Union, an eager audience ready to be inspired, and stepping into the spotlight is none other than President Yoweri Museveni. With a flourish, he begins his oration, invoking the spirit of African unity, the dream of a continent free from the vestiges of colonialism, and the promise of a future where all African nations stand shoulder to shoulder in solidarity. It's enough to make one believe that Museveni himself might just be the reincarnation of Kwame Nkrumah or Patrice Lumumba.

But let's not get carried away. For all his eloquence and impassioned pleas, Museveni's Pan-Africanist showmanship is nothing more than a carefully crafted illusion. Like a seasoned illusionist, he knows precisely how to direct the audience's attention away from the uncomfortable truths lurking backstage. While he speaks of unity and liberation, his actions tell a story of division and repression.

Take, for instance, his favorite trope: the emancipation of Africa from neo-colonial chains. Oh, the fervor with which he decries the evils of Western influence, the exploitation of African resources, and the subjugation of its people. He paints a vivid picture of a continent shackled by economic imperialism, yearning to break free and reclaim its destiny. And who better to lead this charge than Museveni, the self-styled liberator?

Yet, as the applause echoes through the halls, one can't help but notice the irony. While he lambasts foreign powers for meddling in Africa's affairs, his own regime has been remarkably adept at forging cozy relationships with those very same powers. Military aid, development assistance, and investment deals flow into Uganda, all while Museveni waxes lyrical about African self-reliance. It's a delicate balancing act, one that requires a deft hand and a willingness to play both sides of the geopolitical chessboard.

And then there's the matter of African solidarity. Museveni's speeches are peppered with references to the brotherhood of African nations, the shared struggles, and the collective triumphs. He speaks of a united Africa, where borders are mere lines on a map, and the bonds of kinship transcend national boundaries. It's a beautiful vision, one that tugs at the heartstrings and stirs the soul.

However, in the cold light of day, Museveni's commitment to this ideal appears rather selective. His treatment of the Banyarwanda people within Uganda's borders stands as a stark testament to the gap between his rhetoric and reality. Despite their deep roots in Ugandan society, the Banyarwanda have found themselves marginalized, their citizenship questioned, and their loyalty doubted. It's a classic case of "us versus them," a convenient scapegoating of a community that has dared to excel and rise within the ranks.

Museveni's Pan-Africanism, it seems, is an exclusive club, one that extends a warm welcome to those who pose no threat to his power but slams the door on those who might challenge his authority. It's a far cry from the inclusive, all-encompassing unity he so passionately preaches. Instead, it's a divisive, self-serving interpretation that serves his political ends while cloaked in the language of liberation.

But let's not overlook the pièce de résistance of his performance: the grand vision of a united Africa. Ah, what a splendid dream! An Africa where all nations are united in purpose, where economic and political barriers dissolve, and where the continent's vast potential is fully realized. Museveni paints a picture so compelling, it's almost possible to forget the myriad challenges and contradictions that lie beneath the surface.

Yet, for all his talk of unity, Museveni's actions have often been more about consolidating his own power than fostering genuine collaboration. His meddling in the affairs of neighboring countries, his support for rebel movements when it suits his agenda, and his selective approach to regional alliances all point to a leader more interested in his own survival than in the lofty ideals of Pan-Africanism.

In the end, Museveni's Pan-Africanism is a masterclass in political theater. It's a carefully constructed narrative designed to project an image of a visionary leader while diverting attention from the inconvenient truths of his regime. It's a performance that has dazzled many, but as the applause dies down and the stage lights dim, one is left to ponder the reality behind the rhetoric. For in the great drama of Pan-Africanism, Museveni is the quintessential pretender, a master illusionist whose greatest trick is convincing the world that he is something he is not.

CHAPTER 2

The 1995 Constitution – A Masterpiece of Exclusion

Now, let's take a closer look at President Museveni's magnum opus, the 1995 Constitution. A document that, in theory, should be a testament to his commitment to equality and justice. Instead, it's a brilliant piece of work if your aim is to disguise xenophobia under the veneer of legality. The indigenous Banyarwanda, despite their longstanding presence in Uganda and their undeniable contribution to its history, found themselves stripped of their citizenship rights. Why? Because they had the audacity to excel, to rise in the military ranks, and to exhibit brilliance that made someone uncomfortable.

Ah, the 1995 Constitution. Heralded as a triumph of democratic principles, this document was supposed to mark a new era for Uganda, an era of inclusivity, fairness, and justice. But as with many things under Museveni's rule, appearances can be deceiving. The Constitution, while adorned with the language of equality, harbors within it the seeds of exclusion and discrimination.

Let's begin with the preamble. It speaks grandly of the sovereign will of the people, of justice and liberty for all Ugandans. It's a stirring introduction, one that promises a bright future. However, as one delves deeper into its articles and clauses, the discrepancies start to emerge. It's almost as if Museveni's legal drafters took inspiration from George Orwell's "Animal Farm": all Ugandans are equal, but some are more equal than others.

The most glaring example of this Orwellian twist lies in the treatment of the Banyarwanda. Despite their integral role in Uganda's society, history, and even in Museveni's own rise to power, the Constitution cleverly excludes them from the full rights of citizenship. It's a masterstroke of legal sophistry. The Banyarwanda, many of whom have lived in Uganda for generations, suddenly found their status as citizens called into question. Why, you ask? Because they excelled. Because they rose through the military ranks. Because they dared to be brilliant in a way that threatened the comfort zones of those in power.

Article after article, the Constitution sets forth criteria that subtly, yet effectively, marginalize the Banyarwanda. It's a brilliant maneuver – disenfranchise a whole group under the guise of legal reform. The legalese is dense enough to confuse the average citizen but clear enough to ensure that those in the know understand exactly who is being targeted.

Consider the requirements for citizenship. The Constitution outlines stringent conditions, including proof of descent and lengthy residency requirements, that are disproportionately difficult for the Banyarwanda to meet. It's a classic bait and switch: offer the promise of inclusion, then set the bar so high that few can actually reach it. And if anyone dares to challenge this exclusion, well, the Constitution is right there, enshrining these barriers in the very fabric of the law.

Moreover, the 1995 Constitution brilliantly employs the tactic of ambiguity. Certain clauses are vague enough to allow for selective interpretation, giving those in power the leeway to apply the law as they see fit. When the Banyarwanda seek to assert their rights, they are met with a bureaucratic labyrinth designed to frustrate and exhaust. It's a Kafkaesque nightmare where the rules are ever-changing, and the goalposts are always moving.

The brilliance of this constitutional framework is its ability to provide a façade of legality to what is essentially state-sponsored xenophobia. By embedding exclusionary practices within the Constitution, Museveni has ensured that his discriminatory policies carry the weight of law. It's a masterclass in how to institutionalize bigotry while maintaining the appearance of democracy and justice.

Yet, the real genius lies in the plausible deniability it affords Museveni. When confronted with accusations of xenophobia, he can point to the Constitution and claim that he is merely upholding the law. It's a perfect shield, one that deflects criticism and obscures the underlying prejudice. Critics are left floundering, trying to navigate the murky waters of legal jargon, while Museveni continues his reign unchallenged.

This exclusionary masterpiece also serves another crucial function: it consolidates Museveni's power by eliminating potential threats. The Banyarwanda, with their military prowess and strategic acumen, represent a formidable force. By stripping them of citizenship, Museveni not only diminishes their influence but also sends a clear message to other would-be challengers: cross me, and you will be erased from the national narrative.

But let's not overlook the irony here. Museveni, the self-proclaimed champion of Pan-Africanism, the great unifier, has crafted a constitution that divides and discriminates. It's a testament to his political acumen that he can speak so passionately about African unity while enacting policies that fracture his own nation. It's as if he has taken Machiavelli's "The Prince" and added his own chapter on the art of constitutional exclusion.

In the end, the 1995 Constitution stands as a monument to Museveni's dual nature: the visionary leader and the cunning strategist. It embodies the contradiction at the heart of his rule – the lofty rhetoric of unity and the harsh reality of division. It is, indeed, a masterpiece of exclusion, one that will be studied by political scientists and legal scholars for years to come as an example of how to enshrine discrimination within the framework of democracy.

The 1995 Constitution of Uganda: Article 9 and the Third Schedule

The 1995 Constitution of Uganda is a comprehensive document that lays out the fundamental laws and principles governing the country. Among its many provisions, Article 9 and the Third Schedule stand out for their implications on citizenship and the recognition of indigenous communities. These sections are particularly relevant in understanding the legal status and treatment of the Banyarwanda, a group that, despite being recognized as indigenous, faces significant discrimination.

Article 9 of the 1995 Constitution

Article 9 of the 1995 Constitution of Uganda is primarily concerned with the acquisition of citizenship. It outlines the various ways through which one can become a citizen of Uganda. These include citizenship by birth, registration, and naturalization. The article sets the framework for who is considered a Ugandan citizen and the processes involved in acquiring this status.

The Third Schedule

*The **Third Schedule** of the Constitution provides a detailed list of Uganda's indigenous communities as of 1st February 1926. This list is crucial because it officially recognizes the various ethnic groups that were present in Uganda at that historical point in time. Among the communities listed in the Third Schedule are the Banyarwanda, acknowledging their long-standing presence and integral role in the country's history.*

Article 10(a) and the Recognition of Indigenous Communities

*Article **10(a)** is closely linked to the Third Schedule, as it specifically states that citizenship can be acquired by birth if one belongs to any of the indigenous communities as recognized in the Third Schedule. This means that the Banyarwanda, being listed among these communities, should have an unequivocal right to Ugandan citizenship by virtue of their historical presence in the country.*

Discrimination Against the Banyarwanda

Despite the constitutional recognition, the Banyarwanda in Uganda face systemic discrimination and exclusion. This contradiction between constitutional rights and actual treatment raises serious concerns about the implementation of the law and the principles of justice and equality in Uganda.

Historical Context

The Banyarwanda have lived in Uganda for generations, contributing significantly to its social, economic, and political landscape. Their inclusion in the Third Schedule of the Constitution as of 1st February 1926 underscores their established presence and indigenous status. However, historical and political factors have led to their marginalization.

Legal and Social Challenges

Citizenship and Documentation*: Many Banyarwanda struggle to obtain essential documents such as national ID cards and passports. Despite the constitutional provisions, bureaucratic hurdles and discriminatory practices often impede their ability to prove their citizenship.*

Political Marginalization*: The Banyarwanda are frequently excluded from political processes and decision-making. This marginalization is a significant barrier to their participation in the governance of Uganda and their ability to advocate for their rights.*

Social Stigmatization*: The Banyarwanda often face social stigma and are portrayed as outsiders or foreigners, despite their deep-rooted history in Uganda. This stigmatization fuels discrimination in various aspects of life, including employment, education, and access to public services.*

The Gap Between Law and Practice

The stark difference between the constitutional provisions and the lived realities of the Banyarwanda highlights a critical gap in the application of the law. While the Constitution of Uganda provides a robust framework for the recognition and inclusion of indigenous communities, the failure to uphold these principles in practice undermines the spirit of the Constitution.

Need for Reforms

To bridge this gap, several measures need to be taken:

Strengthening Legal Enforcement*: There must be a concerted effort to ensure that the constitutional provisions regarding citizenship and the recognition of indigenous communities are enforced effectively. This includes simplifying the processes for obtaining documentation and removing discriminatory barriers.*

Political Inclusion*: Efforts should be made to include the Banyarwanda in political processes and decision-making bodies. This can help ensure that their voices are heard and their interests are represented at all levels of government.*

Public Awareness and Education*: Campaigns to raise awareness about the constitutional rights of the Banyarwanda and other indigenous communities can help combat social stigma and promote inclusivity. Education systems should incorporate the history and contributions of these communities to foster a more inclusive national identity.*

Monitoring and Accountability*: Establishing independent bodies to monitor the implementation of constitutional provisions and hold government agencies accountable can help address issues of discrimination and ensure compliance with the law.*

Conclusion

The 1995 Constitution of Uganda, through Article 9, the Third Schedule, and Article 10(a), provides a clear legal foundation for the recognition and inclusion of the Banyarwanda as indigenous citizens. However, the persistent discrimination they face indicates a failure to translate these legal provisions into reality. Bridging this gap requires comprehensive legal, political, and social reforms aimed at ensuring that the rights enshrined in the Constitution are upheld and that all Ugandans, regardless of their ethnic background, are treated with dignity and respect.

And so, as we turn the page on this chapter, let us remember that behind the grand speeches and the stirring declarations lies a legal document that speaks volumes about the true nature of Museveni's Pan-Africanism. It is a document that reveals the depths of his political cunning and the extent of his ambition. It is, in short, the quintessential expression of the Great Pan-African Pretender.

CHAPTER 3

Xenophobia in the Age of Pan-Africanism

But wait, isn't Pan-Africanism all about unity, regardless of tribal or national origins? It appears our President missed that memo. The Banyarwanda were simply too good, too smart, and too close to power for his liking. So, what better way to neutralize a threat than to deny their very existence as citizens? It's a classic maneuver – paint them as outsiders, question their loyalty, and voila, problem solved.

Welcome to the age of Pan-Africanism, where unity is preached from every podium and celebrated in grand summits, yet the reality on the ground tells a different story. It's a time when the rhetoric of inclusivity is at its peak, but the actions of leaders reveal an undercurrent of division and exclusion. At the forefront of this paradox is Uganda's President Yoweri Museveni, a man who has masterfully wielded the tools of xenophobia while donning the cloak of Pan-Africanism.

Let's delve deeper into this masterclass in political sleight of hand. The Banyarwanda, an ethnic group with deep historical roots in Uganda, found themselves in the crosshairs of Museveni's exclusionary policies. Despite their significant contributions to the nation's development and their longstanding presence, they became the convenient scapegoat in a game of political chess. Why? Because they were competent, ambitious, and, most importantly, a potential threat to Museveni's grip on power.

It's an age-old tactic, really. When faced with a group that excels and poses a challenge to the status quo, the easiest way to undermine them is to question their legitimacy. By painting the Banyarwanda as outsiders, Museveni effectively created a narrative that cast doubt on their loyalty and right to belong. It's a narrative steeped in fear and suspicion, designed to rally the majority against a fabricated enemy.

Imagine, if you will, the President's inner circle huddled in a dimly lit room, plotting their next move. The Banyarwanda, with their increasing influence and military acumen, are discussed in hushed tones. They are too successful, too integrated, too powerful. Something must be done. And so, the plan is hatched: strip them of their citizenship, question their allegiance, and turn the populace against them. It's Machiavellian politics at its finest.

The execution of this plan is nothing short of a political masterstroke. Through a series of legal maneuvers, the Banyarwanda are slowly but surely pushed to the fringes of society. Their citizenship is revoked, their loyalty is questioned, and their identity is systematically erased. All of this is done under the guise of legality, with the Constitution providing the perfect cover for these exclusionary tactics.

But Museveni doesn't stop there. He amplifies the rhetoric, using his platform to stoke the flames of xenophobia. In speech after speech, he subtly reinforces the idea that the Banyarwanda are not truly Ugandan, that their loyalties lie elsewhere. It's a campaign of misinformation and propaganda, designed to sow doubt and distrust among the populace. And, as history has shown, once a seed of doubt is planted, it can grow into a formidable force of division.

The irony, of course, is that this exclusionary practice stands in stark contrast to the very principles of Pan-Africanism that Museveni so ardently champions. Pan-Africanism, in its truest form, is about breaking down barriers, fostering unity, and celebrating the diversity of the African continent. It's about recognizing that the artificial borders imposed by colonialism should not define us, and that our shared heritage and common struggles bind us together as one people.

Yet, Museveni's brand of Pan-Africanism seems to be highly selective. It's a version that celebrates unity in theory but practices exclusion in reality. It's a vision that extols the virtues of solidarity while simultaneously undermining the very fabric of national cohesion. The Banyarwanda, with their rich history and undeniable contributions, should be celebrated as part of Uganda's mosaic. Instead, they are vilified and marginalized.

This dichotomy between rhetoric and reality is not unique to Uganda. Across the continent, we see leaders who pay lip service to the ideals of Pan-Africanism while engaging in practices that divide their people. It's a convenient hypocrisy, one that allows them to maintain a façade of progressivism while entrenching their own power. The Banyarwanda's plight is a microcosm of this broader trend, a stark reminder that the journey towards true unity is fraught with obstacles.

In Museveni's Uganda, the Banyarwanda's exclusion serves multiple purposes. It not only neutralizes a potential threat but also provides a handy scapegoat for the nation's problems. Whenever the government faces criticism for corruption, economic mismanagement, or human rights abuses, it can deflect attention by pointing to the "foreign" element within. It's a distraction technique as old as politics itself – blame the outsider, rally the populace, and maintain control.

But this strategy comes at a cost. The social fabric of Uganda is weakened, trust between communities is eroded, and the true potential of the nation remains unrealized. The very principles that could propel Uganda towards greatness – unity, inclusivity, and mutual respect – are sacrificed on the altar of political expediency.

As we conclude this chapter, let us reflect on the lessons to be learned from this age of Pan-Africanism tinged with xenophobia. True unity requires more than just eloquent speeches and grand declarations; it demands genuine inclusivity and the courage to embrace diversity. It calls for leaders who not only preach the ideals of Pan-Africanism but live by them, ensuring that all citizens, regardless of their origins, are treated with dignity and respect.

The Banyarwanda's struggle is a testament to the resilience of a people who refuse to be erased. It is a call to action for all who believe in the true spirit of Pan-Africanism – a spirit that transcends borders, celebrates our common humanity, and strives for a future where every African can thrive.

CHAPTER 4

The Art of Deflection

Deflection is an art, and our President is a maestro. When cornered about his domestic failures – the rampant corruption, the mismanagement of resources, the lack of basic services – he pulls out the Pan-African card. It's a tried and true tactic: shift the focus from his shortcomings by pontificating about the broader struggle of the African continent. Who has time to question his leadership when there's a grand vision to chase?

President Yoweri Museveni has honed the skill of deflection to perfection, turning it into a high art form. Whenever his administration's incompetence or corruption comes under scrutiny, he skillfully shifts the narrative to grandiose visions of Pan-African unity. The beauty of this tactic lies in its simplicity and effectiveness. By redirecting the public's attention from immediate, pressing issues to the broader, nobler cause of African solidarity, Museveni manages to evade accountability time and time again.

Take, for instance, the issue of rampant corruption. Under Museveni's watch, corruption has become entrenched in Ugandan society, permeating every level of government and public service. Funds meant for healthcare, education, and infrastructure mysteriously vanish, lining the pockets of the well-connected. Public officials, emboldened by a culture of impunity, engage in brazen acts of graft, knowing full well that the chances of facing repercussions are slim.

Yet, when confronted with these scandals, Museveni's response is predictable. Instead of addressing the corruption head-on, he delivers impassioned speeches about the evils of colonialism and the need for African countries to stand united against Western exploitation. It's a narrative that resonates deeply with a populace still grappling with the legacies of colonial rule. But it also conveniently diverts attention away from the President's own failures to tackle the corruption festering within his administration.

The mismanagement of resources is another area where Museveni's deflection tactics come into play. Uganda is blessed with abundant natural resources, from fertile agricultural land to mineral wealth. However, the management of these resources has been nothing short of disastrous. Incompetence and corruption have led to inefficient utilization, environmental degradation, and missed opportunities for sustainable development.

When critics highlight these issues, Museveni once again reaches for his Pan-African playbook. He speaks eloquently about the need for Africa to reclaim control of its resources from neocolonial powers, portraying himself as the vanguard of this struggle. It's a message that stirs nationalist sentiments, but it also glosses over the stark reality that much of Uganda's resource mismanagement is homegrown, a product of his own government's ineptitude and greed.

Then there are the basic services – or rather, the lack thereof. In many parts of Uganda, access to essential services such as healthcare, education, and clean water remains woefully inadequate. Hospitals are underfunded and understaffed, schools lack basic supplies, and infrastructure projects are often abandoned halfway. The ordinary Ugandan struggles daily with the consequences of a government that has failed to deliver on its most fundamental responsibilities.

Faced with these glaring deficiencies, Museveni deftly pivots the conversation. He frames these issues within the context of Africa's broader struggle for independence and self-sufficiency. He talks about the importance of building a Pan-African identity, of working together to overcome the legacy of colonialism. It's an inspiring vision, but it does little to address the immediate needs of the Ugandan people who are left wondering when their President will focus on the here and now.

Museveni's deflection tactics are not limited to speeches and rhetoric. He also employs strategic distractions to keep the public preoccupied with other matters. When scandals or crises threaten to expose his administration's failures, he often orchestrates high-profile events or initiates controversial policies to shift the public's focus. For example, during times of heightened scrutiny, he might announce ambitious infrastructure projects or engage in military ventures that dominate the headlines, pushing stories of corruption and mismanagement to the back pages.

This art of deflection has allowed Museveni to maintain his grip on power despite a litany of failures that would have toppled lesser leaders. By consistently redirecting the narrative to the grand struggle of Pan-Africanism, he has managed to create a buffer against criticism. His ability to intertwine his personal legacy with the broader narrative of African unity ensures that any attack on his leadership is framed as an attack on the Pan-African ideal itself.

However, this tactic comes at a significant cost. The deflection of attention from domestic issues to Pan-African rhetoric means that the urgent needs of the Ugandan people are often neglected. The focus on grand visions of continental unity diverts resources and political will away from addressing the very real and pressing problems within Uganda. The result is a populace that continues to suffer from poor public services, corruption, and mismanagement, all while being asked to buy into a vision of unity that remains largely abstract.

Moreover, Museveni's use of Pan-Africanism as a shield against criticism undermines the genuine potential of the Pan-African movement. By co-opting its ideals for personal and political gain, he risks discrediting the very concept of African unity in the eyes of those who see through his deflection. True Pan-Africanism requires honest leadership, accountability, and a commitment to improving the lives of all Africans, not just using it as a convenient cover for domestic failures.

As we move forward in this exploration of Museveni's rule, it becomes clear that his mastery of deflection is both his greatest strength and his most significant weakness. While it has allowed him to navigate the treacherous waters of Ugandan politics, it has also prevented him from addressing the core issues that plague his country. In the end, the art of deflection may be Museveni's most enduring legacy – a testament to his skill as a politician, but also a stark reminder of the unmet promises and unfulfilled potential of his tenure.

CHAPTER 5

The Convenient Scapegoat

The Banyarwanda are a convenient scapegoat. They speak a language similar to those beyond Uganda's borders, so it's easy to paint them as perpetual foreigners. Never mind that their roots in Uganda run deep, deeper than some of the President's own policies. By stoking fears of the 'other', he diverts attention from the real issues. It's a neat trick – keep the populace preoccupied with an invented enemy while he continues his reign unchecked.

In the complex political landscape of Uganda, the Banyarwanda have become the perfect target for President Museveni's scapegoating tactics. Their linguistic and cultural ties to Rwanda make them an easy group to otherize, despite their long-standing presence and contributions to Ugandan society. This deliberate alienation serves a dual purpose: it distracts the populace from the government's failures and consolidates Museveni's power by creating a common enemy.

The contributions of prominent figures like Fred Rwigyema and Paul Kagame, both of whom played crucial roles in Museveni's rise to power, highlight the profound irony of this scapegoating. Rwigyema and Kagame, alongside many other Banyarwanda, were instrumental in the National Resistance Army (NRA) struggle that brought Museveni to power in 1986. Their military prowess and strategic acumen were indispensable in the liberation efforts, yet the community they represent finds itself marginalized and ostracized in Museveni's Uganda.

Fred Rwigyema, a revered military leader, and Paul Kagame, who would later become the President of Rwanda, were key allies in Museveni's fight against the oppressive regimes that preceded his rule. Their sacrifices and leadership were pivotal in the NRA's success.

However, instead of honoring their legacy by embracing the Banyarwanda as an integral part of Uganda's fabric, Museveni has chosen to reciprocate their contributions with exclusion and suspicion.

This betrayal is not just a historical footnote; it is an ongoing reality for many Banyarwanda who live in Uganda. They are systematically stripped of their rights and subjected to scrutiny and discrimination. Their loyalty is questioned, and their citizenship is often denied, relegating them to the status of perpetual outsiders. It's a cruel irony that those who helped shape Uganda's political landscape are now being erased from its narrative.

Museveni's strategy of using the Banyarwanda as scapegoats is a calculated move to divert attention from pressing domestic issues. When corruption scandals surface, when public services falter, and when resources are mismanaged, the narrative shifts to the supposed threat posed by the Banyarwanda. This tactic taps into deep-seated fears and prejudices, providing a convenient distraction from the government's shortcomings.

The President's rhetoric often paints the Banyarwanda as infiltrators, subtly suggesting that their true allegiance lies with Rwanda rather than Uganda. This narrative is further fueled by the geopolitical tensions between Uganda and Rwanda, which Museveni exploits to stoke nationalist sentiments. By framing the Banyarwanda as a fifth column, he galvanizes support among other ethnic groups, consolidating his base while deflecting criticism of his administration.

This tactic of creating an internal enemy is not new; it has been employed by many leaders throughout history to maintain control. By focusing the populace's anger and frustration on a marginalized group, Museveni diverts potential dissent and keeps the populace preoccupied with an invented enemy. It's a classic divide-and-conquer strategy, one that has proven effective time and again.

However, this approach has severe consequences for the social fabric of Uganda. It fosters an environment of mistrust and hostility, pitting communities against each other. The Banyarwanda, despite their deep roots and significant contributions, are alienated and marginalized. This not only undermines social cohesion but also hinders the nation's progress by excluding a group that has much to offer.

The narrative of the Banyarwanda as perpetual foreigners ignores the rich history and deep connections they have with Uganda. Many Banyarwanda families have lived in Uganda for generations, contributing to its cultural, economic, and social development. Their exclusion is not just an injustice to them but a disservice to the entire nation.

Moreover, the scapegoating of the Banyarwanda reflects a broader trend of xenophobia and exclusion that runs counter to the ideals of Pan-Africanism. True Pan-Africanism calls for unity and solidarity among all African peoples, transcending ethnic and national boundaries. Museveni's use of Pan-African rhetoric, while practicing exclusion at home, exposes the hollowness of his commitment to these ideals.

As we move forward, it is crucial to recognize the damaging effects of scapegoating and exclusion on Uganda's development. The contributions of the Banyarwanda, from leaders like Rwigyema and Kagame to ordinary citizens, should be acknowledged and celebrated. Building a truly inclusive society requires moving beyond the politics of fear and division and embracing the diversity that strengthens the nation.

In conclusion, Museveni's use of the Banyarwanda as a convenient scapegoat is a deliberate and cynical strategy to maintain his grip on power. It diverts attention from his administration's failures and exploits ethnic tensions for political gain. However, this approach not only betrays the legacy of those who fought alongside him but also undermines the principles of unity and inclusion that are essential for Uganda's progress. It is time to move beyond scapegoating and work towards a future where all Ugandans, regardless of their origins, are valued and respected.

CHAPTER 6

Betraying the Banyarwanda

The Banyarwanda are a convenient scapegoat. They speak a language similar to those beyond Uganda's borders, so it's easy to paint them as perpetual foreigners. Never mind that their roots in Uganda run deep, deeper than some of the President's own policies. By stoking fears of the 'other', he diverts attention from the real issues. It's a neat trick – keep the populace preoccupied with an invented enemy while he continues his reign unchecked.

In the complex political landscape of Uganda, the Banyarwanda have become the perfect target for President Museveni's scapegoating tactics. Their linguistic and cultural ties to Rwanda make them an easy group to otherize, despite their long-standing presence and contributions to Ugandan society. This deliberate alienation serves a dual purpose: it distracts the populace from the government's failures and consolidates Museveni's power by creating a common enemy.

The contributions of prominent figures like Fred Rwigyema and Paul Kagame, both of whom played crucial roles in Museveni's rise to power, highlight the profound irony of this scapegoating. Rwigyema and Kagame, alongside many other Banyarwanda, were instrumental in the National Resistance Army (NRA) struggle that brought Museveni to power in 1986. Their military prowess and strategic acumen were indispensable in the liberation efforts, yet the community they represent finds itself marginalized and ostracized in Museveni's Uganda.

Fred Rwigyema, a revered military leader, and Paul Kagame, who would later become the President of Rwanda, were key allies in Museveni's fight against the oppressive regimes that preceded his rule. Their sacrifices and leadership were pivotal in the NRA's success.

However, instead of honoring their legacy by embracing the Banyarwanda as an integral part of Uganda's fabric, Museveni has chosen to reciprocate their contributions with exclusion and suspicion.

This betrayal is not just a historical footnote; it is an ongoing reality for many Banyarwanda who live in Uganda. They are systematically stripped of their rights and subjected to scrutiny and discrimination. Their loyalty is questioned, and their citizenship is often denied, relegating them to the status of perpetual outsiders. It's a cruel irony that those who helped shape Uganda's political landscape are now being erased from its narrative.

Museveni's strategy of using the Banyarwanda as scapegoats is a calculated move to divert attention from pressing domestic issues. When corruption scandals surface, when public services falter, and when resources are mismanaged, the narrative shifts to the supposed threat posed by the Banyarwanda. This tactic taps into deep-seated fears and prejudices, providing a convenient distraction from the government's shortcomings.

The President's rhetoric often paints the Banyarwanda as infiltrators, subtly suggesting that their true allegiance lies with Rwanda rather than Uganda. This narrative is further fueled by the geopolitical tensions between Uganda and Rwanda, which Museveni exploits to stoke nationalist sentiments. By framing the Banyarwanda as a fifth column, he galvanizes support among other ethnic groups, consolidating his base while deflecting criticism of his administration.

This tactic of creating an internal enemy is not new; it has been employed by many leaders throughout history to maintain control. By focusing the populace's anger and frustration on a marginalized group, Museveni diverts potential dissent and keeps the populace preoccupied with an invented enemy. It's a classic divide-and-conquer strategy, one that has proven effective time and again.

However, this approach has severe consequences for the social fabric of Uganda. It fosters an environment of mistrust and hostility, pitting communities against each other. The Banyarwanda, despite their deep roots and significant contributions, are alienated and marginalized. This not only undermines social cohesion but also hinders the nation's progress by excluding a group that has much to offer.

The narrative of the Banyarwanda as perpetual foreigners ignores the rich history and deep connections they have with Uganda. Many Banyarwanda families have lived in Uganda for generations, contributing to its cultural, economic, and social development. Their exclusion is not just an injustice to them but a disservice to the entire nation.

Moreover, the scapegoating of the Banyarwanda reflects a broader trend of xenophobia and exclusion that runs counter to the ideals of Pan-Africanism. True Pan-Africanism calls for unity and solidarity among all African peoples, transcending ethnic and national boundaries. Museveni's use of Pan-African rhetoric, while practicing exclusion at home, exposes the hollowness of his commitment to these ideals.

As we move forward, it is crucial to recognize the damaging effects of scapegoating and exclusion on Uganda's development. The contributions of the Banyarwanda, from leaders like Rwigyema and Kagame to ordinary citizens, should be acknowledged and celebrated. Building a truly inclusive society requires moving beyond the politics of fear and division and embracing the diversity that strengthens the nation.

In conclusion, Museveni's use of the Banyarwanda as a convenient scapegoat is a deliberate and cynical strategy to maintain his grip on power. It diverts attention from his administration's failures and exploits ethnic tensions for political gain. However, this approach not only betrays the legacy of those who fought alongside him but also undermines the principles of unity and inclusion that are essential for Uganda's progress. It is time to move beyond scapegoating and work towards a future where all Ugandans, regardless of their origins, are valued and respected.

write and extend the following: Chapter 6: Betraying the Banyarwanda One cannot overlook the profound irony that President Museveni's rise to power was paved by the sacrifices of the very people he now marginalizes. The Banyarwanda of Uganda, whose strategic brilliance and loyalty played a crucial role in his ascent, now find themselves betrayed. Fearing their astuteness and potential challenge to his authority, Museveni and his henchmen chose to exclude them from citizenry. It's a textbook example of biting the hand that feeds you.

CHAPTER 7

Betraying the Banyarwanda again

One cannot overlook the profound irony that President Museveni's rise to power was paved by the sacrifices of the very people he now marginalizes. The Banyarwanda of Uganda, whose strategic brilliance and loyalty played a crucial role in his ascent, now find themselves betrayed. Fearing their astuteness and potential challenge to his authority, Museveni and his henchmen chose to exclude them from citizenship. It's a textbook example of biting the hand that feeds you.

The Crucial Role of the Banyarwanda

In the annals of Uganda's political history, the Banyarwanda are indelibly etched as pivotal players in Museveni's journey to power. During the guerrilla warfare of the early 1980s, the Banyarwanda, including notable figures like Fred Rwigyema and Paul Kagame, were indispensable. Their strategic acumen, unwavering loyalty, and exceptional military prowess provided the backbone for the National Resistance Army's (NRA) successful campaign against the oppressive regimes of Milton Obote and Idi Amin.

Rwigyema and Kagame, alongside their compatriots, were not mere foot soldiers; they were key strategists and leaders. Rwigyema's charisma and leadership inspired many, while Kagame's strategic brilliance became evident in numerous battles. These individuals did not just fight for Museveni; they believed in the promise of a new Uganda, one that would be just and inclusive, a stark contrast to the regimes they were fighting to overthrow.

The Irony of Exclusion

Yet, as Museveni consolidated his power, the very people who had been instrumental in his rise found themselves increasingly marginalized. The irony is staggering: those who once shared the trenches with Museveni, dreaming of a better future for all Ugandans, are now treated as second-class citizens. The Banyarwanda, despite their deep roots in Ugandan society and their undeniable contributions, are systematically excluded from full citizenship.

The betrayal is not just political but deeply personal. Many Banyarwanda who fought alongside Museveni did so with the expectation that their sacrifices would lead to a more inclusive and just Uganda. Instead, they find themselves on the fringes, their loyalty questioned, and their contributions overlooked. Museveni, it seems, fears their astuteness and potential to challenge his authority. By excluding them, he seeks to neutralize any perceived threats to his continued rule.

Legal and Social Marginalization

The exclusion of the Banyarwanda is not merely a matter of rhetoric but is entrenched in legal and social policies. The 1995 Constitution, heralded as a new dawn for Uganda, contains provisions that effectively strip many Banyarwanda of their citizenship. These legal barriers are compounded by social discrimination, where the Banyarwanda are often depicted as outsiders, despite their long-standing presence in the country.

This marginalization serves multiple purposes. It allows Museveni to solidify his power by removing a potential source of opposition while also diverting attention from his administration's failures. By painting the Banyarwanda as perpetual foreigners, he stokes nationalist sentiments that distract the populace from issues like corruption, poor public services, and economic mismanagement.

The Cost of Betrayal

The cost of this betrayal is immense, not just for the Banyarwanda but for Uganda as a whole. By excluding a significant and talented portion of the population, Uganda deprives itself of the skills, knowledge, and dedication that the Banyarwanda bring. This exclusion undermines national unity, creating a divided society where trust and collaboration are eroded.

Furthermore, the treatment of the Banyarwanda undermines the very principles of justice and equality that Museveni once purported to champion. It is a stark reminder that political expediency often trumps ideals in the corridors of power. The betrayal of the Banyarwanda is not just a historical footnote but a present reality that continues to affect lives and communities.

The Path Forward

For Uganda to truly progress, it must reckon with this betrayal. Acknowledging the contributions of the Banyarwanda and rectifying the injustices they face is crucial. This requires both legal reforms to restore their citizenship and social initiatives to foster inclusion and unity.

Moreover, Museveni's administration must move beyond the politics of fear and division. True leadership would involve recognizing the mistakes of the past and making concerted efforts to build an inclusive society where all Ugandans, regardless of their ethnic background, are valued and respected.

Conclusion

In the grand narrative of Museveni's rule, the betrayal of the Banyarwanda stands out as a particularly egregious act of political expediency. It is a betrayal not just of a people but of the very ideals that Museveni once claimed to uphold. As Uganda looks to the future, it must confront this dark chapter and strive to create a nation where the sacrifices and contributions of all its people are recognized and celebrated. Only then can the wounds of the past begin to heal, and a truly inclusive and just Uganda emerge.

CHAPTER 8

Stateless in Their Own Land

Imagine being born in a country, living there for 50 years, contributing to its society, and then suddenly being declared stateless. That's the harsh reality for many Banyarwanda in Uganda. Denied passports and national ID cards, they exist in a limbo, remembered only when it's convenient for the President – like during elections, where their votes are needed to legitimize his grip on power. It's a cruel game, one that speaks volumes about the hollow nature of his Pan-African rhetoric.

The Reality of Statelessness

For the Banyarwanda in Uganda, the concept of citizenship has become a cruel illusion. Despite generations of residence and substantial contributions to the nation's development, they find themselves denied the most basic rights and recognition. This state-imposed statelessness is not just a bureaucratic oversight; it is a calculated strategy to disenfranchise a community perceived as a threat to the ruling regime.

Denied passports, national ID cards, and other essential documents, the Banyarwanda are effectively rendered invisible. They cannot travel, vote, or access many public services. Their existence is acknowledged only when it serves the interests of those in power, particularly during election seasons. At such times, their votes are courted to lend legitimacy to a regime that otherwise marginalizes them. This selective recognition underscores the cynical manipulation at play, where a disenfranchised community is exploited for political gain.

Living in Limbo

The Banyarwanda's lives in Uganda are characterized by a perpetual state of uncertainty and insecurity. Without proper identification, they face numerous challenges in their daily lives. They struggle to secure employment, access healthcare, and enroll their children in school. Basic activities that most Ugandans take for granted become insurmountable obstacles for the stateless Banyarwanda.

This limbo status also exposes them to constant harassment and exploitation. Without legal protection, they are vulnerable to arbitrary arrests, detention, and extortion by law enforcement officials. Their lack of documentation makes them easy targets for those seeking to abuse their power. The fear of being detained or deported hangs over their heads, adding to the psychological burden of statelessness.

The Election Gambit

During election periods, the Banyarwanda suddenly become visible again. Political operatives descend upon their communities, promising recognition and benefits in exchange for their votes. These empty promises are a stark reminder of their utility to the regime: not as valued citizens, but as pawns in a larger political game. After the elections, the promises evaporate, and the Banyarwanda return to their marginalized existence, their temporary utility forgotten.

This cycle of exploitation and abandonment highlights the profound hypocrisy of the ruling regime. Museveni's government, which professes to uphold Pan-African values of unity and inclusion, reveals its true nature in its treatment of the Banyarwanda. The selective acknowledgment of their existence during elections is a testament to the transactional nature of the regime's relationship with this community.

The Human Cost

The human cost of statelessness is immense. Families are torn apart as individuals seek refuge in neighboring countries where they might find recognition and stability. The constant uncertainty takes a toll on mental health, with many experiencing depression and anxiety. The social fabric of the Banyarwanda community is frayed as they navigate a system that refuses to acknowledge their humanity.

The younger generation is particularly affected. Deprived of proper education and opportunities, their potential is stifled. They grow up with a sense of alienation and frustration, aware of their heritage but denied the right to claim it fully. This systemic exclusion not only robs them of their present but also dims the prospects for their future.

The Hollow Rhetoric of Pan-Africanism

Museveni's Pan-African rhetoric rings hollow in the face of the Banyarwanda's plight. True Pan-Africanism is about embracing diversity, fostering unity, and ensuring that all Africans, regardless of their ethnic or national origins, can live with dignity and respect. The treatment of the Banyarwanda starkly contradicts these ideals, revealing a regime more interested in maintaining power than in realizing the vision of a united Africa.

The President's speeches about African solidarity and liberation are undermined by his actions at home. The exclusion of the Banyarwanda exposes the duplicity of his administration, which uses the language of unity while practicing division. It is a clear demonstration that the principles of Pan-Africanism are being co-opted for political expediency rather than genuinely pursued.

A Call to Action

Addressing the statelessness of the Banyarwanda requires a concerted effort from both the Ugandan government and the international community. Legal reforms are essential to grant citizenship rights to those who have been unjustly denied them. This includes revising the 1995 Constitution and implementing policies that recognize the historical presence and contributions of the Banyarwanda.

Beyond legal recognition, there must be a shift in societal attitudes. The narrative that paints the Banyarwanda as perpetual foreigners must be challenged and dismantled. Education and awareness campaigns can play a crucial role in fostering understanding and acceptance. Building a more inclusive society requires acknowledging past wrongs and making amends.

The international community also has a role to play. Advocacy and pressure from human rights organizations can highlight the issue on the global stage, holding the Ugandan government accountable for its actions. Support for initiatives that promote citizenship rights and social inclusion can help bring about meaningful change.

Conclusion

The plight of the Banyarwanda in Uganda is a stark reminder of the gap between rhetoric and reality in the pursuit of Pan-African ideals. Their statelessness is a grave injustice that demands urgent attention. Recognizing their contributions, granting them citizenship, and integrating them fully into Ugandan society are not just moral imperatives but essential steps towards realizing a truly united and inclusive Africa. As Uganda navigates its future, it must confront the injustices of the past and strive to build a nation where all its people can thrive with dignity and respect.

CHAPTER 9

Voices of Resistance

Brave individuals like Frank Gashumba have been at the forefront, calling for reforms and justice. Yet, their efforts are met with deaf ears and, often, retribution. Gashumba's activism shines a light on the President's duplicity, but change remains elusive. The struggle of the Banyarwanda is a stark reminder that Pan-Africanism, under Museveni, is nothing more than a facade.

The Courage of Activism

In the face of systemic oppression and marginalization, it takes immense courage to stand up and demand justice. Frank Gashumba, a prominent Ugandan activist and advocate for the rights of the Banyarwanda, embodies this courage. Through his relentless efforts, Gashumba has become a symbol of resistance against the injustices perpetuated by Museveni's regime. His activism is not just a fight for the Banyarwanda but a broader call for human rights, transparency, and genuine democratic governance in Uganda.

Gashumba's journey has been fraught with challenges. He has faced harassment, intimidation, and threats from the state apparatus designed to silence dissent. Despite these risks, he continues to speak out, using his platform to expose the contradictions and failings of the government. His message resonates with many who are disillusioned with the status quo, inspiring a growing movement for change.

Shining a Light on Duplicity

Gashumba's activism has been particularly effective in highlighting the duplicity of President Museveni. While Museveni proclaims his commitment to Pan-African ideals and unity, Gashumba exposes the stark reality of exclusion and division. Through social media campaigns, public speeches, and grassroots mobilization, he has brought international attention to the plight of the Banyarwanda and the broader issues of governance in Uganda.

By documenting and publicizing instances of abuse and discrimination, Gashumba has painted a vivid picture of the daily struggles faced by the Banyarwanda. His work underscores the disconnect between Museveni's rhetoric and his policies, revealing a leader who is more interested in maintaining power than in fostering true unity and justice. Gashumba's efforts have made it increasingly difficult for the regime to hide behind the veneer of Pan-Africanism.

The Price of Activism

The price of such activism is high. Gashumba, like many other activists, has faced severe reprisals. State security forces frequently target him and his family, and he has been subjected to arbitrary arrests and detentions. These actions are meant to intimidate him and others who dare to challenge the government. Yet, Gashumba remains undeterred, driven by a deep sense of justice and a vision for a better Uganda.

Other activists, too, have joined the struggle, facing similar risks. Their stories of resilience and courage add to the growing chorus demanding change. Together, they form a network of resistance that, despite the repression, continues to push for reforms and justice. This network is a testament to the enduring spirit of those who refuse to accept oppression as their fate.

The Broader Movement for Change

Gashumba's fight is part of a larger movement that seeks to address not only the rights of the Banyarwanda but also the broader issues of governance and human rights in Uganda. This movement includes civil society organizations, human rights defenders, and ordinary citizens who are fed up with corruption, mismanagement, and injustice. They demand a government that is accountable, transparent, and truly representative of all its people.

The movement faces significant obstacles. Museveni's regime has shown a willingness to use all means at its disposal to suppress dissent. This includes deploying security forces to break up protests, enacting draconian laws to stifle free speech, and manipulating electoral processes to maintain power. Despite these challenges, the movement persists, drawing strength from the resilience of its members and the righteousness of their cause.

The Facade of Pan-Africanism

The struggle of the Banyarwanda, as highlighted by Gashumba and other activists, lays bare the facade of Pan-Africanism under Museveni. True Pan-Africanism calls for unity, equality, and justice for all Africans, regardless of their ethnic or national origins. Museveni's version, however, is selective and self-serving, using the language of Pan-Africanism to cloak policies of exclusion and repression.

This hypocrisy is not lost on the international community. Human rights organizations and foreign governments have increasingly called out the Ugandan government for its human rights abuses and lack of genuine democratic practices. While these calls often fall on deaf ears, they add to the growing pressure on Museveni's regime to change its ways.

The Path Forward

The path forward is fraught with difficulties, but it is also filled with hope. The voices of resistance, though currently marginalized, continue to gain strength. The growing awareness and solidarity within and outside Uganda offer a glimmer of hope for a future where justice and equality prevail.

To support this movement, it is crucial for the international community to continue applying pressure on the Ugandan government. Sanctions, diplomatic interventions, and support for civil society can help create an environment where activists like Gashumba can operate more freely and effectively. Additionally, efforts to document and expose abuses must be sustained, ensuring that the world remains aware of the situation in Uganda.

Within Uganda, it is essential for the movement to remain united and resilient. Building alliances across ethnic and political lines can strengthen the push for reform. Engaging in non-violent resistance, leveraging social media, and continuing to educate and mobilize the populace are key strategies that can help bring about change.

Conclusion

The voices of resistance, led by brave individuals like Frank Gashumba, represent the best hope for a just and inclusive Uganda. Their struggle against a regime that uses Pan-African rhetoric to mask its duplicity is a powerful reminder of the ongoing fight for human rights and true democracy. While the road ahead is challenging, the determination and courage of these activists offer a beacon of hope for a future where all Ugandans can live with dignity and justice.

CHAPTER 10

The East African Political Federation – A Pipe Dream?

Museveni's grand vision of a political federation of East Africa rings hollow when one considers his treatment of the Banyarwanda. How can he expect to be taken seriously about creating a united East Africa when he persecutes a significant indigenous community within his own borders? True unity starts at home, and his failure to protect the rights of all Ugandans undermines any genuine efforts towards regional integration.

The Vision of East African Unity

President Yoweri Museveni has long championed the idea of an East African Political Federation, a bold vision that would see countries like Uganda, Kenya, Tanzania, Rwanda, and Burundi merging into a single political entity. This federation is intended to foster economic growth, political stability, and collective security, presenting a united front in an increasingly globalized world. Museveni's speeches on this topic are filled with grandiose language about unity, shared heritage, and common destiny.

The potential benefits of such a federation are significant. A united East Africa could leverage its collective resources, negotiate more effectively on the global stage, and enhance regional infrastructure and trade. The idea is not without merit, and many see it as a natural progression for a region with shared cultural and historical ties.

The Hypocrisy of Internal Disunity

However, Museveni's vision for regional unity is starkly contradicted by his actions at home. His persecution of the Banyarwanda within

Uganda undermines any claim he might have to being a unifier. The Banyarwanda, despite their deep roots in Uganda, face systemic discrimination and exclusion under his regime. This hypocrisy does not go unnoticed by neighboring countries and the international community, casting doubt on Museveni's sincerity and ability to lead a broader regional integration effort.

How can Museveni credibly advocate for the unity of East African nations while simultaneously marginalizing a significant ethnic community within his own borders? True unity cannot be achieved through exclusion and repression. The treatment of the Banyarwanda is a glaring example of the dissonance between Museveni's rhetoric and reality, and it raises serious questions about his commitment to the principles of equality and justice that a political federation would require.

The Role of Human Rights in Regional Integration

For any political federation to succeed, it must be built on a foundation of respect for human rights and the rule of law. Museveni's record in these areas is highly problematic. The marginalization of the Banyarwanda is just one aspect of a broader pattern of human rights abuses, including the suppression of political dissent, curtailment of free speech, and arbitrary detentions. These actions erode trust and cooperation, both within Uganda and with its neighbors.

Regional integration requires mutual respect and a commitment to shared values. Museveni's actions suggest that he is more interested in consolidating his power than in fostering genuine unity. His approach to governance, characterized by divisiveness and repression, is antithetical to the cooperative spirit needed for a successful political federation.

Economic Disparities and Integration

Economic disparities between East African countries also pose significant challenges to the idea of a political federation. While some nations have made strides in economic development, others lag behind, exacerbated by poor governance and corruption. Museveni's Uganda, despite its potential, struggles with significant economic mismanagement and corruption, which further undermines the credibility of his vision for regional integration.

For a federation to work, there must be a concerted effort to address these disparities and promote equitable development. Museveni's track record does not inspire confidence in his ability to lead such an effort. The systemic issues within Uganda, including the marginalization of communities like the Banyarwanda, indicate a lack of commitment to the inclusive economic policies that are essential for regional stability and prosperity.

Building Trust and Cooperation

Trust is the cornerstone of any successful political federation. Museveni's treatment of the Banyarwanda has severely damaged trust within Uganda, and it has broader implications for his relationships with neighboring countries. Rwanda, in particular, has a vested interest in the treatment of the Banyarwanda, given the shared ethnic ties. Museveni's policies have strained relations with Rwanda, highlighting the difficulties of fostering regional cooperation when internal disunity prevails.

Building a political federation requires more than just lofty speeches; it demands tangible actions that promote inclusivity, justice, and cooperation. Museveni's failure to address the grievances of the Banyarwanda and other marginalized groups within Uganda undermines the trust needed to build such a federation. Without addressing these internal issues, his vision for East African unity remains a pipe dream.

The Importance of Leadership and Vision

Effective leadership is critical for the success of any regional integration effort. Museveni's leadership, marked by authoritarian tendencies and disregard for human rights, poses a significant obstacle to the realization of a political federation. True leadership would involve addressing internal disparities, fostering inclusivity, and promoting genuine democratic governance. Unfortunately, Museveni's actions suggest that he is more focused on maintaining his grip on power than on laying the groundwork for a united East Africa.

For the East African Political Federation to become a reality, it requires leaders who embody the values of unity, equality, and justice. It demands a departure from the politics of exclusion and repression. Museveni's current approach falls short of these ideals, casting doubt on his ability to lead such a transformative initiative.

Conclusion

Museveni's grand vision of a political federation of East Africa remains an elusive dream, undermined by his own actions and policies. The persecution of the Banyarwanda within Uganda starkly contradicts his calls for regional unity, revealing a deep hypocrisy that cannot be ignored. True unity starts at home, and Museveni's failure to protect the rights of all Ugandans undermines any genuine efforts towards regional integration.

For the dream of an East African Political Federation to be realized, it requires leaders who are committed to the principles of inclusivity, justice, and human rights. It demands a genuine effort to address internal disparities and build trust and cooperation among nations. Until Museveni addresses the contradictions in his own governance, his vision for a united East Africa will remain a pipe dream. The path to regional integration is complex and challenging, but it begins with ensuring that all citizens, regardless of their ethnic background, are treated with dignity and respect.

CHAPTER 11

The Reality Check

So, how does one reconcile the lofty ideals of Pan-Africanism with the exclusionary practices of Uganda's President? It's simple: you don't. The rhetoric of Pan-African unity is a smokescreen, a distraction from the failures at home. True Pan-Africanism would mean embracing all Africans, protecting their rights, and valuing their contributions regardless of their ethnic background. It would mean recognizing the Banyarwanda as rightful citizens and contributors to the nation's fabric.

The Smokescreen of Rhetoric

President Museveni's speeches are often adorned with grandiose declarations about African unity, liberation from neo-colonial chains, and the dream of a united Africa. To the untrained ear, these might sound like the words of a visionary leader committed to the betterment of the continent. However, beneath this veneer lies a starkly different reality – one where exclusion, repression, and division are the order of the day.

Museveni's rhetoric serves a dual purpose. Domestically, it acts as a smokescreen, diverting attention from pressing issues such as corruption, poor public services, and human rights abuses. Internationally, it paints a picture of a progressive leader, masking the systemic injustices perpetuated under his rule. This dual strategy has allowed Museveni to maintain a semblance of legitimacy both at home and abroad.

The Reality of Exclusion

The Banyarwanda, a community deeply woven into the fabric of Uganda's history and society, have borne the brunt of this exclusionary policy. Despite their significant contributions, they are often depicted as outsiders, their loyalty questioned, and their rights denied. This treatment is not an isolated phenomenon but part of a broader strategy to consolidate power by marginalizing potential threats.

True Pan-Africanism, in its essence, is about inclusivity, unity, and mutual respect. It recognizes that Africa's strength lies in its diversity and that every ethnic group, every individual, has a role to play in the continent's development. Museveni's exclusionary practices stand in direct contradiction to these principles, revealing the hollowness of his Pan-African rhetoric.

The Failure to Embrace Diversity

To genuinely embody Pan-African ideals, Museveni would need to embrace and protect the rights of all Ugandans, including the Banyarwanda. This would mean acknowledging their contributions, granting them full citizenship rights, and integrating them into the national narrative. It would mean moving beyond the politics of division and fostering a sense of national unity that transcends ethnic boundaries.

However, Museveni's actions suggest that he is unwilling to take these steps. The marginalization of the Banyarwanda is a symptom of a broader unwillingness to embrace diversity and inclusivity. This failure not only undermines the principles of Pan-Africanism but also hampers Uganda's progress as a nation.

The Illusion of Progress

Museveni's regime often touts economic growth and infrastructural development as evidence of progress. While it is true that Uganda has seen some economic advancements, these benefits are unevenly distributed, often concentrated among the elite while the majority, including marginalized communities like the Banyarwanda, continue to struggle.

Moreover, economic progress cannot be measured solely in terms of GDP growth or infrastructure. It must also include social progress, human rights, and the well-being of all citizens. The exclusion and marginalization of any group signify a deeper societal failure, one that economic metrics alone cannot mask.

The Path to Genuine Pan-Africanism

To move towards true Pan-Africanism, Uganda must address these systemic injustices. This requires a fundamental shift in policy and attitude, starting with the recognition of the Banyarwanda as rightful citizens. It involves implementing legal and social reforms to protect their rights, promote their inclusion, and celebrate their contributions.

Such a shift would also necessitate addressing the broader issues of governance that plague Uganda. Corruption, lack of transparency, and human rights abuses must be tackled head-on. This would involve strengthening institutions, promoting accountability, and ensuring that the rule of law is upheld for all citizens, not just a select few.

The Role of Civil Society

Civil society has a crucial role to play in this transformation. Activists, human rights organizations, and ordinary citizens must continue to demand justice and accountability. Their voices are essential in highlighting the discrepancies between Museveni's rhetoric and reality and in pushing for the reforms needed to achieve true inclusivity.

International support can also be instrumental. By applying pressure on the Ugandan government to uphold human rights and embrace democratic principles, the international community can help create an environment conducive to change. However, this support must be consistent and principled, avoiding the pitfalls of selective outrage and geopolitical interests.

Conclusion

The reality check for Museveni's Pan-African rhetoric reveals a stark contrast between words and actions. True Pan-Africanism is about more than just speeches and declarations; it is about creating a society where every individual, regardless of their ethnic background, is valued and included. For Uganda, this means recognizing the Banyarwanda as integral members of the nation, protecting their rights, and addressing the broader issues of governance and justice.

As long as Museveni continues to use Pan-Africanism as a smokescreen for exclusionary practices, the dream of a united Africa will remain just that – a dream. It is time for Uganda to take concrete steps towards genuine inclusivity and justice, setting an example for the continent and proving that true Pan-Africanism is more than just rhetoric. Only then can the lofty ideals of unity and solidarity become a reality for all Africans.

CHAPTER 12

A Call for Genuine Pan-Africanism

The time has come to call out this charade. Pan-Africanism should not be a convenient cover for xenophobia or a tool for political maneuvering. It should be a genuine movement towards unity, justice, and equality. The Banyarwanda deserve their rightful place in Uganda, not as foreigners in their own land, but as integral members of the nation's mosaic. Only then can we start talking about true Pan-Africanism.

Unmasking the Charade

For too long, the rhetoric of Pan-Africanism has been used as a smokescreen to mask exclusionary and xenophobic policies. Leaders like President Museveni have exploited the noble ideals of unity and solidarity to advance their political agendas while systematically marginalizing certain groups. This hypocrisy undermines the very foundation of Pan-Africanism and betrays the trust of those who genuinely believe in the movement's potential.

The True Essence of Pan-Africanism

True Pan-Africanism is rooted in the principles of unity, justice, and equality. It envisions a continent where all Africans, regardless of their ethnic or national origins, are valued and respected. It calls for the dismantling of artificial borders created by colonial powers and the forging of a collective identity based on shared history and common aspirations. To achieve this vision, we must confront and address the internal contradictions that hinder our progress.

Embracing Diversity

At the heart of genuine Pan-Africanism is the recognition and celebration of Africa's diversity. This means acknowledging the contributions of all ethnic groups and ensuring that no community is marginalized or excluded. The Banyarwanda, with their rich cultural heritage and significant contributions to Uganda's development, deserve to be recognized as integral members of the nation. Their exclusion not only undermines their rights but also weakens the social fabric of Uganda.

Building an Inclusive Society

Creating an inclusive society requires a multifaceted approach. Legal and policy reforms are essential to guarantee the rights of all citizens, including the Banyarwanda. This involves revising discriminatory laws, providing equal access to resources and opportunities, and ensuring that all voices are heard in the political process. Beyond legal measures, there must be a concerted effort to foster social cohesion and mutual respect among different communities.

The Role of Education

Education plays a crucial role in shaping attitudes and fostering inclusivity. A curriculum that emphasizes the values of unity, diversity, and human rights can help build a more inclusive society. By teaching young people about the history and contributions of all ethnic groups, we can promote understanding and tolerance. Schools should be spaces where diversity is celebrated and where students learn the importance of solidarity and justice.

The Power of Civil Society

Civil society organizations and grassroots movements are instrumental in advocating for genuine Pan-Africanism. Activists, human rights defenders, and community leaders must continue to raise awareness about the issues of exclusion and marginalization. Their efforts are vital in holding governments accountable and pushing for the necessary reforms. By building alliances and mobilizing support, civil society can drive the movement towards true unity and justice.

International Solidarity

The struggle for genuine Pan-Africanism is not confined to national borders. International solidarity is essential in supporting the efforts of activists and promoting human rights across the continent. Global organizations, foreign governments, and diaspora communities can play a significant role in advocating for change. By highlighting issues of exclusion and discrimination on international platforms, we can apply pressure on governments to uphold the principles of Pan-Africanism.

Moving Beyond Rhetoric

To move beyond rhetoric, leaders must demonstrate their commitment to Pan-Africanism through concrete actions. This means not only addressing internal issues of discrimination and exclusion but also fostering regional cooperation and integration. True Pan-Africanism requires a collective effort to tackle the challenges facing the continent, from economic disparities to political instability. By working together, African nations can build a future based on shared prosperity and mutual respect.

The Future of Pan-Africanism

The future of Pan-Africanism depends on our ability to embrace its true essence. It calls for a collective commitment to justice, equality, and unity. As we move forward, we must ensure that the principles of Pan-Africanism are reflected in our policies, our institutions, and our everyday interactions. The dream of a united Africa can only be realized when all Africans are included and valued.

Conclusion

The time has come to call out the charade of using Pan-Africanism as a cover for exclusion and political maneuvering. True Pan-Africanism is a genuine movement towards unity, justice, and equality. The Banyarwanda and all marginalized groups deserve their rightful place in Uganda and across the continent. Only by embracing diversity, fostering inclusivity, and upholding the principles of justice can we build a united and prosperous Africa. It is time to move beyond rhetoric and work towards making the ideals of Pan-Africanism a reality for all Africans.

CHAPTER 13

The Crossroads of Choice

To all Banyarwanda speakers in Uganda, the time has come to make a choice. Instead of begging for what is rightfully yours, there are two clear paths before you. The first is to withdraw your investments, your wealth, and relocate them to Rwanda. There, you can request citizenship and rebuild your lives in a country where your heritage and contributions will be valued and respected.

The second path is more arduous but deeply rooted in the principles of justice and equality. Stand up and fight for what belongs to you. Organize, mobilize, and demand the recognition and rights that are yours by birth and by contribution. Let your voices be heard loudly and clearly. This fight is not just for your own dignity, but for the future generations of Banyarwanda who deserve to be recognized as full citizens of Uganda.

The Path of Relocation

The first option for the Banyarwanda is to leave behind a land that has marginalized and persecuted them and start anew in Rwanda. This path, while painful, offers a fresh start in a nation where their heritage is not just acknowledged but celebrated. Rwanda, under the leadership of many who understand the plight of the Banyarwanda in Uganda, offers a place where they can rebuild their lives with dignity and respect.

Relocating to Rwanda means transferring investments, assets, and skills to a country that values their contributions. It means participating in a society that sees them as integral members, not outsiders. For many, this path offers a sense of immediate relief and acceptance, providing a stable environment to grow and thrive.

However, this option also comes with its own set of challenges. Uprooting lives, leaving behind homes and communities, and starting over in a new country is not an easy decision. It involves emotional, financial, and logistical hurdles. Yet, for those who choose this path, it promises a life free from the constant threat of discrimination and statelessness.

The Path of Resistance

The second path, while more challenging, is rooted in the fight for justice and equality. It involves staying in Uganda and demanding the rights and recognition that the Banyarwanda deserve as rightful citizens. This path calls for organizing, mobilizing, and advocating for change. It requires building a movement that can challenge the status quo and push for legal and social reforms.

Standing up for justice means engaging in activism, forming alliances with other marginalized groups, and leveraging both local and international support. It involves using legal channels to challenge discriminatory practices, participating in political processes, and raising awareness about the Banyarwanda's plight. This path is about fighting for a future where all Ugandans, regardless of their ethnic background, are treated with dignity and respect.

Organizing for Change

To effectively organize and mobilize, the Banyarwanda must build a strong, united front. This involves creating networks of support within the community, identifying leaders who can articulate their demands, and developing strategies to engage with the broader Ugandan society. Grassroots activism, community meetings, and social media campaigns can all play a role in amplifying their voices.

Forming alliances with civil society organizations, human rights groups, and sympathetic political entities can strengthen the movement. These alliances can provide resources, expertise, and platforms to advocate for change. By working together, the Banyarwanda can build a coalition that is capable of challenging systemic discrimination and pushing for inclusive policies.

Leveraging International Support

International support can be a powerful tool in the fight for justice. By drawing attention to the Banyarwanda's situation on the global stage, they can pressure the Ugandan government to enact reforms. Engaging with international human rights organizations, foreign governments, and the United Nations can help highlight their plight and mobilize global advocacy.

Petitions, reports, and international campaigns can raise awareness and generate support for the Banyarwanda's cause. Diplomatic interventions and economic sanctions can also be leveraged to push the Ugandan government towards recognizing and protecting the rights of all its citizens.

The Importance of Education and Awareness

Education and awareness are critical components of this struggle. By educating both the Banyarwanda and the broader Ugandan society about the history, contributions, and rights of the Banyarwanda, the movement can combat misinformation and prejudice. Schools, universities, and community centers can serve as venues for spreading knowledge and fostering dialogue.

Public awareness campaigns, media outreach, and cultural events can also help change perceptions and build support. Highlighting the stories of Banyarwanda who have contributed to Uganda's development can humanize their struggle and counter the narrative of exclusion.

Building a Future for Generations to Come

The fight for recognition and rights is not just about the present generation; it is about securing a future for the generations to come. Ensuring that the Banyarwanda children grow up in a society that values and respects them is a crucial goal. This means advocating for inclusive policies in education, healthcare, and employment, and creating opportunities for young Banyarwanda to thrive.

By standing up and fighting for justice, the Banyarwanda can pave the way for a more inclusive and equitable Uganda. Their struggle can inspire other marginalized communities and contribute to building a nation that truly embodies the principles of equality and justice.

Conclusion

The crossroads of choice presents two paths for the Banyarwanda in Uganda. Whether they choose to relocate to Rwanda or to stay and fight for their rights, both paths require courage and resilience. The decision is deeply personal and will depend on individual circumstances and convictions.

Regardless of the path chosen, the Banyarwanda's struggle is a powerful reminder of the need for genuine Pan-Africanism, one that embraces diversity, protects rights, and values contributions. By standing together and advocating for change, they can transform their plight into a movement for justice and equality, not just for themselves but for all marginalized communities in Uganda and beyond.

The time for action is now. The Banyarwanda have the power to shape their destiny and to fight for a future where they are recognized as full citizens of Uganda. Their journey will be challenging, but with unity, determination, and support, they can achieve the justice and equality they deserve.

EPILOGUE: THE FUTURE OF PAN-AFRICANISM

As we look to the future, let's hope for a version of Pan-Africanism that lives up to its name. One that celebrates diversity, fosters inclusion, and truly works for the betterment of all Africans. Uganda's President has shown us what Pan-Africanism is not. Now, it's up to us to redefine what it should be. Whether by choosing to build anew in Rwanda or by standing firm in Uganda, the Banyarwanda have the power to shape their destiny. And in doing so, they can pave the way for a genuine Pan-African movement that embraces all Africans.

Redefining Pan-Africanism

The concept of Pan-Africanism has always held the promise of a united, prosperous Africa, free from the remnants of colonialism and internal strife. However, as we have seen, leaders like President Museveni have often twisted this noble idea to serve their political ends, creating divisions rather than fostering unity. True Pan-Africanism must transcend rhetoric and be grounded in actions that promote justice, equality, and mutual respect.

To redefine Pan-Africanism, we must start by addressing the internal contradictions that undermine its principles. This means recognizing and celebrating the diverse ethnic, cultural, and linguistic identities that make up the African continent. It involves creating inclusive societies where all individuals have equal opportunities to contribute to and benefit from national development.

The Role of the Banyarwanda

The Banyarwanda's struggle for recognition and rights in Uganda is a microcosm of the broader challenges facing Pan-Africanism. Their journey, whether it leads them to rebuild in Rwanda or to continue their fight in Uganda, serves as a powerful example of resilience and determination. By standing up for their rights, the Banyarwanda can inspire other marginalized communities across Africa to demand justice and equality.

Their efforts can also highlight the importance of regional solidarity. The support and advocacy from other African nations and the diaspora can play a crucial role in amplifying their voices and pressuring the Ugandan government to enact reforms. The Banyarwanda's fight is not just about their community; it is about setting a precedent for how all Africans should be treated with dignity and respect.

Building Inclusive Nations

For Pan-Africanism to thrive, African nations must commit to building inclusive societies. This involves not only legal and policy reforms but also a shift in societal attitudes. Governments must prioritize the protection of human rights, the promotion of social justice, and the eradication of discrimination in all its forms. Education systems should teach the values of unity, diversity, and mutual respect, preparing future generations to uphold these principles.

Economic policies should also aim to reduce disparities and ensure that all citizens, regardless of their background, have access to opportunities and resources. By fostering inclusive economic growth, African nations can create a more equitable and prosperous continent.

The Power of Regional Integration

Regional integration is a cornerstone of Pan-Africanism. Strengthening political, economic, and cultural ties between African countries can help address common challenges and leverage shared opportunities. Initiatives such as the African Continental Free Trade Area (AfCFTA) and regional economic communities (RECs) can promote trade, investment, and cooperation, benefiting all member states.

However, true regional integration requires more than just economic agreements. It demands a commitment to human rights, good governance, and the rule of law. African leaders must work together to create a political and social environment that supports regional integration and ensures that its benefits are felt by all citizens.

The Role of the Diaspora

The African diaspora also has a vital role to play in the future of Pan-Africanism. Diaspora communities can act as bridges between Africa and the rest of the world, advocating for African interests and contributing to development through remittances, investment, and knowledge transfer. By engaging with diaspora organizations and leveraging their expertise, African nations can enhance their development efforts and strengthen their global presence.

Embracing a New Vision

As we look to the future, we must embrace a new vision of Pan-Africanism that is inclusive, just, and transformative. This vision requires the active participation of all Africans, both on the continent and in the diaspora. It calls for leaders who are committed to the principles of unity, equality, and justice, and who are willing to take bold actions to uphold these values.

The journey towards genuine Pan-Africanism will not be easy, but it is a journey worth undertaking. By learning from the past and addressing the challenges of the present, we can build a future where all Africans can thrive. The Banyarwanda's struggle is a reminder of the work that remains to be done, but it is also a testament to the power of resilience and hope.

Conclusion

The future of Pan-Africanism lies in our ability to create societies that celebrate diversity, foster inclusion, and work for the betterment of all Africans. The Banyarwanda have shown us the importance of standing up for justice and equality, and their journey can inspire us all to strive for a more united and prosperous Africa. Whether by building anew in Rwanda or standing firm in Uganda, their actions pave the way for a Pan-African movement that truly embraces all Africans.

It is up to us to redefine Pan-Africanism and make it a reality. By committing to the principles of unity, justice, and equality, we can build a future where every African is valued and respected. The time for action is now, and together, we can create a continent that lives up to the ideals of Pan-Africanism and ensures a brighter future for all.

A Warning to Uganda: The Perils of Segregation

When people are continuously segregated and marginalized, they inevitably seek strength in self-preservation. This search for survival and dignity can lead to organized resistance, which, if the situation is poorly handled, can spiral into conflict. Uganda stands at a critical juncture where its treatment of the Banyarwanda and other marginalized communities can either pave the way for unity and progress or precipitate a descent into turmoil reminiscent of the M23 crisis in the Democratic Republic of Congo (DRC).

Historical Context: The M23 Crisis

The M23 rebellion in the DRC, led predominantly by the marginalized Banyamulenge community, serves as a stark reminder of what can happen when systemic discrimination and exclusion are left unaddressed. The Banyamulenge, despite their long-standing presence in the DRC, faced severe persecution, exclusion from political processes, and violent attacks. These injustices fueled resentment and eventually led to the formation of the M23 rebel group, which sought to fight for their rights and protect their community.

Drawing Parallels to Uganda

Uganda's treatment of the Banyarwanda bears unsettling similarities to the plight of the Banyamulenge. The Banyarwanda, recognized as an indigenous community under the 1995 Constitution, still face significant barriers to obtaining citizenship, political representation, and social acceptance. This continued marginalization threatens to ignite a similar cycle of resistance and conflict.

The Danger of Ignoring Injustice

Ignoring the legitimate grievances of the Banyarwanda and other marginalized groups can lead to severe consequences:

Escalation of Tensions: Persistent discrimination fosters anger and resentment, which can escalate into organized resistance. As seen with the M23, marginalized groups may eventually resort to armed struggle if they feel there is no peaceful path to justice and recognition.

Regional Instability: Conflicts that arise from internal marginalization can spill over borders, affecting regional stability. The M23 crisis not only destabilized the DRC but also had significant repercussions for neighboring countries. Uganda could face similar regional fallout if internal conflicts escalate.

Humanitarian Crisis: Armed conflicts lead to significant humanitarian crises, including displacement, loss of lives, and destruction of livelihoods. The international community's response to such crises often comes at a high cost, both in terms of resources and human suffering.

Economic Consequences: Sustained internal conflict can severely damage a country's economy. Investment drops, tourism dwindles, and resources are diverted from development to military expenditure. Uganda's economic progress could be derailed if marginalized communities take up arms in response to continued exclusion.

The Call to Action

To prevent a potential crisis, Uganda must take immediate and decisive steps:

Address Grievances: The government must engage in meaningful dialogue with marginalized communities like the Banyarwanda. Listening to their grievances and addressing them through legal and policy reforms is crucial for fostering inclusion.

Promote Inclusivity: Ensuring that all communities have equal access to citizenship, political representation, and social services is vital. This includes revising discriminatory laws and practices that prevent marginalized groups from fully participating in society.

Foster Unity: Public campaigns that promote national unity and the value of diversity can help change societal attitudes. Educating the broader public about the contributions and rights of all ethnic groups can reduce stigma and foster a more inclusive national identity.

Strengthen Institutions: Building strong, independent institutions that uphold the rule of law and human rights is essential. These institutions should be empowered to address discrimination and hold perpetrators accountable.

Monitor and Act: Continuous monitoring of the situation is necessary to ensure that reforms are being implemented effectively. The government should be prepared to act swiftly to prevent any signs of escalating tensions.

Conclusion

Uganda stands at a crossroads. The treatment of the Banyarwanda and other marginalized communities will significantly shape the nation's future. By choosing the path of inclusion, justice, and unity, Uganda can avoid the fate of the DRC and the M23 crisis. However, ignoring these issues risks plunging the country into a similar cycle of conflict and instability.

The time to act is now. By addressing the legitimate grievances of marginalized communities and fostering a genuinely inclusive society, Uganda can pave the way for lasting peace and prosperity. The consequences of inaction are too dire to contemplate. Let this be a call to all Ugandans to work towards a future where every citizen, regardless of their ethnic background, can thrive in dignity and equality.

Don't miss out!

Visit the website below and you can sign up to receive emails whenever Kayumba David publishes a new book. There's no charge and no obligation.

https://books2read.com/r/B-A-KRSOC-TURHF

BOOKS2READ

Connecting independent readers to independent writers.

Did you love *Harvesting Illusions: The Global Greed and the Pan-African Paradox*? Then you should read *Bridging the Rift: A Pacifist Vision for the Israel-Palestine Future*[1] by Kayumba David!

This book envisions a way forward through a unique confederation model—a path not dependent on dominance but on coexistence, not on division but on shared governance. This confederation is a structure that respects the autonomy and self-determination of each community while fostering cooperation on shared issues. It allows both Israel and Palestine to maintain their own governance, culture, and identity, yet provides a framework through which they can work together as neighbors, partners, and ultimately, as a shared community.

In a world that has seen enough of war and division, a new chapter of humility and hope is required. True peace, as pacifist theologian

---

1. https://books2read.com/u/bxk81d

2. https://books2read.com/u/bxk81d

Stanley Hauerwas reminds us, is not merely the absence of conflict but the presence of justice, respect, and mutual understanding. Hauerwas writes, "The work of peace is nothing less than the work of worship." Peace is not a passive state but an active practice, a deliberate commitment to see and honor each other as human beings made in the image of God. It requires humility to set aside pride and past grievances, and it demands courage to extend a hand rather than a fist.

Read more at www.zcews.org.

About the Author

Kayumba David is an accomplished author known for his works that span across themes of spirituality, African experiences, and healthcare chaplaincy. His writings often delve into profound social, political, and personal subjects.

One of his notable works is "Visas: The Irony of Freedom", where he critiques the paradoxes faced by many Africans regarding international travel and freedom

He also authored "Hope and Healing: A Chaplain's Handbook," which reflects on his experiences as a chaplain and emphasizes the importance of compassion and spiritual care in healthcare and prison environments

Kayumba's works reflect his personal journey through theological study and lay ministry, having faced challenges within religious institutions, especially during his time in Belgium, where he became an advocate for open theological debate

His contributions in literature offer insights into African realities, the complexities of modern spirituality, and the role of chaplaincy in emotional healing.

Read more at www.zcews.org.